STUDY GUIDE
to Accompany
SOCIOLOGY
A Core Text

James K. Semones

Library of Congress Cataloging-in-Publication Data

Semones, James K.
    Study guide to accompany Sociology.

    1. Sociology—Examinations—Study guides.   I. Semones,
James K. Sociology. II. Title
HM51.S426 1990 Suppl.   301   89-24673

ISBN: 0-03-028734-0

Address Orders to: 6277 Sea Harbor Drive, Orlando, FL 32887
    1-800-782-4479, or 1-800-433-0001 (in Florida)

Address Editorial Correspondence to: 301 Commerce Street, Suite 3700,
    Fort Worth, TX 76102

Printed in the United States of America

0 1 2 3   016   9 8 7 6 5 4 3 2 1

Holt, Rinehart & Winston, Inc.
The Dryden Press
Saunders College Publishing

Contents

Part One

Study Guide

How to Use The Study Guide

The Study Guide is designed to help you master the material in *Sociology,* 1/ e, for superior performance on exams. As such, it is divided into thirteen sections that correspond to the thirteen chapters in the text. Each section consists of three elements: Desired Learning Outcomes (DLOs), Development of the Comprehensive Outline, and Learning Assessment Test. These elements are designed to be used in conjunction with "Effective Study Skills: A System for Academic Excellence (ESS)," the second part of this learning aid. They are briefly explained as follows:

DESIRED LEARNING OUTCOMES
(DLOs)

Stated at the beginning of each section of the Study Guide, the DLOs provide you with the focus needed to master the material in each chapter. In essence, they represent "what you should know" about each chapter to help you perform well on exams. **These DLOs serve as a preview for use with ESS Step 1.** In addition, your instructor has been provided a manual containing a test bank of questions that may be used on your exams. These questions are keyed to the DLOs stated in this Study Guide.

DEVELOPMENT OF THE COMPREHENSIVE OUTLINE
(USING SKILLS CONTAINED IN ESS STEP 2)

To learn as much as you can, you should outline the material in each chapter you read. Since the mind looks for order, structure, and category, it will more readily grasp material that is concisely and coherently summarized. Outlining is relatively easy, once you know how. In the "Effective Study Skills" (ESS) section, this skill is fully explained under "Textbook Usage Skills" (ESS Step 1). Then, in "Content Organization Skills" (ESS Step 2), you are instructed in how to construct a comprehensive written outline (from all sources of course content) from which to study for each exam. To reinforce mastery of these ESS components, a portion of each chapter in the text has been outlined in the Study Guide to show you how to organize content material for study. *For the best results on exams and for better grades, you should make a comprehensive outline of each textook chapter, plus all material from class lectures and outside readings that is not repeated in the text.* Using this approach, you will have all important material condensed into one source document from which to study for exams.

LEARNING ASSESSMENT TEST
(FOR USE WITH ESS STEP 3)

At the end of each section of the Study Guide is a 25-item learning assessment test. Each test is representative of (1) the material in the chapter it covers (and the stated DLOs) and (2) the items in your instructor's test bank (although the questions are not identical). Therefore, your performance on the learning assessment test should be a good indicator of how well you might perform on an actual exam. Especially when used in conjunction with the ESS system, the learning assessment test is also a good gauge of how well you are progressing with your ESS skills. It is recommended that the day before each exam (see ESS Step 3: "Exam Preparation Skills"), you take the learning assessment tests for all chapters that are to be included.

Chapter 1

The Sociological Perspective

DESIRED LEARNING OUTCOMES
(A PREVIEW FOR USE WITH ESS STEP 1)

After successful study of this chapter, the student should be able to

1. define *sociology* as a concept and discuss its nature;

2. identify and briefly discuss some of the basic areas of specialization within sociology;

3. demonstrate an understanding of the nature of science as a means of explanation;

4. compare and contrast several other means of explanation with science;

5. list and briefly explain the basic characteristics of science;

6. show how theory in science differs from theory in religion and philosophy;

7. compare and contrast the physical sciences with the social sciences;

8. discuss in some detail the expression *sociological imagination;*

9. describe the different types of potential careers that may be pursued with different levels of education in sociology;

10. discuss career prospects in sociology for the future;

11. trace the elements of social thought in Western civilization that ultimately led to the emergence of sociology as a formal discipline in the nineteenth century;

12. summarize the contributions made to social thought (and the ultimate development of sociology) by each of the following persons: Socrates, Plato, Aristotle, Khaldun, and Montesquieu;

13. identify the man regarded today as the "founding father" of sociology and discuss his contributions;

14. compare and contrast the perspectives and contributions made by each of the four nineteenth-century "masters of sociological thought": Spencer, Durkheim, Marx, and Weber;

15. identify at least one "founding mother" of sociology during the nineteenth or early twentieth century and discuss her contributions;

16. discuss the emergence and development of American sociology during the nineteenth and twentieth centuries; and

17. explain how sociologists analyze human social behavior from each of the following theoretical perspectives: functionalism, conflict theory, and interactionism.

Note: For specific information on how to address the instructions in these DLOs (e.g., "list," "explain," "compare and contrast," etc.), consult pages 107–111 of the ESS supplement that follows this Study Guide.

DEVELOPMENT OF THE COMPREHENSIVE OUTLINE
(USING SKILLS CONTAINED IN ESS STEP 2)

To master the DLOs for Chapter 1, it is recommended that you outline the chapter as explained on pages 92–95 of ESS. The following is an example of what "The Nature of Science" section of the chapter might look like after you have developed your own written outline of it. Since this is the second major heading in the chapter, it is labeled Roman numeral II.

Note: For the student trying to learn the ESS skill of outlining, these outline examples are provided throughout the Study Guide, sometimes in sentence form for the sake of clarity. Once you master ESS, however, your final outline for each exam should consist of brief phrases, abbreviations, and acronyms (that you devise and understand) which should require less than half the space.

II. The Nature of Science

    A. Science as a Means of Explanation
        1. **Science**—an objective and systematic method of observing and explaining reality in a verifiable manner. Explanation: Scientists make no prejudgments about reality and pursue truth wherever it leads them.
        2. The scientific method is based on several assumptions about reality (e. g., phenomena in nature are linked through cause-and-effect relationships) that are included in epistemology. **Epistemology**—an area in the philosophy of science devoted to the study of knowledge and how it is verified.
    B. Other Means of Explanation
        1. *Appeal to authority*—trusting others (e. g., politicians, physicians, teachers) to pro-

vide one with the truth. Can lead to victimization by those who would lie to and exploit others.

2. *Mysticism*—appeal to "supernatural authority" (e. g., faith healers, prophets) or experience. Sometimes a mystical experience is drug induced.
3. *Tradition*—accepting what worked in the past. Can provide security and peace of mind, but can also encourage undue bias and narrow-mindedness.
4. *Religion*—contains elements of authority, mysticism, and tradition. Many different religions. Can be uplifting and satisfying in some cases or used to justify cruelty and exploitation in others.
5. *Philosophy*—a systematic and rational means of organizing thought processes. Originated with the Greeks. A valuable perspective today although lacking in a reliable means of verifying propositions related to human experience.

C. Characteristics of Science
1. *Science is theoretical*—**Scientific theory** consists of clearly stated propositions that have been verified to some degree. In science, "theory" (propositions) and "fact" (verified information) go together, two parts of the same whole. By contrast, "theory" in religion and philosophy often cannot be verified.
2. *Science is empirical*—**Empiricism** represents the manner in which evidence in science is gathered through the organized use of the senses.
3. *Science is objective*—**Objectivity** refers to an unbiased and unprejudiced approach to determining truth. Truth is tentative and subject to change with better evidence. Thus science is open-ended and self-correcting because verification can be replicated by anyone who uses its method.
4. *Science is cumulative*—**Cumulative knowledge** is knowledge that is constantly being added to, modified, and refined. Examples: Recent advances in medicine and flight.

D. Physical Sciences and Social Sciences
1. **Physical sciences** are those that examine the physical and biological world. Examples: biology, chemistry, physics. Characteristics:
   a. are more concrete (with a focus on physical matter)
   b. contain universal laws
   c. examine the unpurposeful actions of matter
2. **Social sciences** are those that examine human behavior. Examples: sociology, psychology, political science. Characteristics:
   a. are more abstract (with a focus on human behavior)
   b. do not contain universal laws
   c. examine the purposeful behavior of human beings

LEARNING ASSESSMENT TEST
(A TEST SIMULATION FOR USE WITH ESS STEP 3)

After completing Step 3 of ESS (Exam Preparation), take this learning assessment test on the material in Chapter 1. The items on this test are representative of the material you need to master and are based directly on the DLOs stated for this chapter.

Part A: Matching

_____ 1. Sociology

_____ 2. Harriet Martineau

_____ 3. *Verstehen*

_____ 4. Institution

_____ 5. Religion

_____ 6. August Comte

_____ 7. Empiricism

_____ 8. Functionalism

_____ 9. Émile Durkheim

_____ 10. Conflict theory

_____ 11. Herbert Spencer

_____ 12. C. Wright Mills

_____ 13. Deduction

_____ 14. Statics

_____ 15. Interactionism

a. Logic that moves from general propositions to specific conclusions

b. Coined the expression "sociological imagination"

c. A sociological perspective that analyzes the parts of society in terms of how they function to promote order and stability

d. Associated with "social Darwinism"

e. The science of individual human behavior

f. The author of the first book written on sociological research methods

g. A sociological perspective that studies the personal meaning people assign to the world around them

h. The science of human social behavior at all levels of society

i. A term used to describe any major structural component of a society

j. A means of explanation that contains elements of authority, mysticism, and tradition

k. Weber's term for empathetic understanding

l. The "father of sociology"

m. The process of sensory investigation through which scientific evidence is gathered

n. The author of *Suicide*, who was the first sociologist to make use of statistical analysis

o. Comte's term for how the elements of society are structured to promote order and stability

p. Originated in large part with the work of Karl Marx

Part B: Multiple Choice

Select the best answer from the choices provided.

16. An unbiased and unprejudiced approach at seeking truth which characterizes science is called
    a. objectivity.
    b. social action.
    c. subjectivity.
    d. epistemology.

17. The sociological perspective that analyzes conflict and power as they relate to social policy and change in society is
   a. the evolutionary perspective.
   b. interactionism.
   c. functionalism.
   d. conflict theory.

18. A researcher who conducts a study on the backgrounds of unwed teenaged mothers would most likely be
   a. a sociologist of education.
   b. an industrial sociologist
   c. a political sociologist.
   d. a family sociologist.

19. The author of the *Republic* who stressed the need for planned societies was
   a. Plato.
   b. Aristotle.
   c. Khaldun.
   d. Parsons.

20. According to August Comte's evolutionary perspective, the stage at which a society is dominated by speculative reasoning or philosophy is the
   a. pretheological stage.
   b. metaphysical stage.
   c. theological stage.
   d. positive stage.

Part C: True or False

21. T F Most graduates with a bachelor's degree in sociology obtain jobs as sociologists.

22. T F Scientific theory differs from theory in religion and philosophy in that it contains objectively verified propositions.

23. T F The Socratic method involves asking penetrating logical questions.

24. T F Induction is a form of logic that involves movement from specific observations of reality to general conclusions or generalizations.

25. T F Unlike the physical sciences, the social sciences contain universal laws pertaining to their subject matter.

Test Answers May Be Found on Page 72.

Percentage Score = (Number of items correct × 4) _____.

Chapter 2

What Sociologists Do: The Research Process

DESIRED LEARNING OUTCOMES
(A PREVIEW FOR ESS STEP 1)

After successful study of this chapter, the student should be able to

1. discuss the two basic types of sociological research; *[handwritten: pure + applied]*

2. list and briefly explain the basic types of *applied sociology*; *[handwritten: applied research, policy research, Clinical Sociology, evaluation research]*

3. list and briefly summarize in chronological order the essential steps normally followed in the completion of a scientific study; *[handwritten: 1. problem 2. Review lit. 3. Form a hypothesis 4. Research design 5. collect data-org. 6. Analyze 7. Report]*

4. explain how the scientific research cycle operates as a process;

5. state the essential purpose of the *research problem* in conducting scientific research; *[handwritten: Spelling out how we will obtain data]*

6. define what is meant by *the review of the literature* in scientific research and show why it is necessary; *[handwritten: See if any studies have been made on the subject]*

7. discuss the *statement of hypotheses* as a step in conducting research; *[handwritten: use logical deduction or Induction]*

10

8. distinguish between an *independent variable* and a *dependent variable;*

   ind. does influencing dependent is influenced

9. define the concept *research design* and identify some of the issues to be examined in deciding which one or ones to use; *1. Surveys 2. experiment 3 Field Research – participant observation*

10. explain at least three different research designs used by sociologists in conducting research, along with possible advantages and potential problems;

11. distinguish between a *cross-sectional study* and a *longitudinal study* in conducting sociological research; *Longitudinal is a single group of people over a period of time. Cross-sect is broad based over a period of time*

12. discuss how the sociologist carries out the stage of sociological research called *analysis of the findings; Statistics significance – summary + presentations. empirical generalizations.*

13. briefly explain how the results of sociological research are reported; *indiv research at libraries, Prof. Journals, Prof. papers at conventions*

14. discuss how the results of sociological research impact on the state of knowlege; and

15. discuss some of the ethical issues faced by those who conduct behavioral research and how sociologists as a professional group have addressed them.

Note: For specific information on how to address the instructions in these DLOs (e. g., "list," "explain," "compare and contrast," etc.), consult pages 107–111 of the ESS supplement that follows this Study Guide.

DEVELOPMENT OF THE COMPREHENSIVE OUTLINE
(USING SKILLS CONTAINED IN ESS STEP 2)

To master the DLOs for Chapter 2, it is recommended that you outline the chapter as explained in ESS. The following is an example of what the "Conducting the Study" section of the chapter might look like after you develop your own written outline of it. Since this is the fourth major heading in the chapter, it is labeled Roman numeral IV.

IV. Conducting the Study

  A. Making Observations (based on research design)
      Consider time frame: How much time will study take?
      1. **Cross-sectional study**—a broad-based study that takes place over a brief period of time (a day or two to a few weeks). Example: Surveys of groups at community, regional, or national levels on one or several issues.
      2. **Longitudinal study**—a study focused on a single group over an extended period of time (often over several years). Example: Tracking a group of schoolchildren over eight or ten years to analyze changes in certain attitudes or behavioral patterns.
  B. Analysis of the Findings (Were hypotheses supported?)
      1. **Statistics**—mathematical procedures that describe the characteristics of variables

and explain or measure the relationships between them (to what extent variables are associated or correlated with one another).

2. Additional aspects of analysis
   a. *.05 level of statistical significance*—a standard used in behavioral research. There must be 5 or fewer chances out of 100 that a statistical correlation between two variables is due to chance for the results to be considered scientifically valid.
   b. *Summary and presentation of the data*—findings placed in tables, graphs, charts, etc.
   c. *Empirical generalizations*—findings derived from a small group (random sample) may be generalized (using induction) to the larger population from which the sample was drawn.

LEARNING ASSESSMENT TEST
(A TEST SIMULATION FOR USE WITH ESS STEP 3)

Part A: Matching

d____ 1. Pure research

h____ 2. Independent variable

k____ 3. Statistics

m____ 4. Survey

m____ 5. Content analysis

p____ 6. Review of the literature

c____ 7. Control group

g____ 8. Population

n____ 9. Sampling error

L____ 10. *Dissertation Abstracts*

e____ 11. Hawthorne effect

f____ 12. Émile Durkheim

a____ 13. Hypothesis

b____ 14. Clinical sociology

i____ 15. Phillip Zimbardo

a. The statement of an expected cause-and-effect relationship between two variables

b. A form of applied sociology

c. In experiment, the group not exposed to independent variable

d. Scientific investigation aimed at expanding the base of knowledge

e. Temporary change in the behavior of people as a result of the presence and influence of outsiders

f. Pioneered modern hypothesis formation and testing in sociology

g. The total group of people being studied

h. The causal or influencing variable

i. A researcher who used an experiment to study the behavior of college students placed in "prison"

j. The effect variable

k. Mathematical procedures used in sociological analysis

l. Where the results of doctoral research in sociology are reported

m. Research design in which the content of communication is studied

n. The degree to which characteristics of a

sample do not represent the population
being studied
o. A research design that involves the use
of a questionnaire
p. An examination of previous research

Part B: Multiple Choice

Select the best answer from the choices provided.

16. When a questionnaire measures what the researcher hopes to measure, it possesses
    a. validity.   c. reliability.
    b. low variability.   d. statistical significance.

17. As indicated by the research of Jane Goodall, John Howard Griffin, and others, the
    most dangerous type of research, in terms of ensuring the personal safety of the investi-
    gator, is
    a. experimental research.   c. participant observation research.
    b. survey research.   d. content analysis research.

18. Sociologist Erving Goffman (1961) "went underground" and took a job as an assistant
    athletic director in a mental hospital in order to "snoop around" undetected and study
    the hospital as a total institution. By doing so, which of the following research designs
    did he use?
    a. The survey.   c. The experiment.
    b. Content analysis.   d. Participant observation.

19. Sociological investigation that examines the consequences of various public policies in
    terms of their degree of effectiveness or ineffectiveness is termed
    a. clinical research.   c. evaluation research.
    b. policy research.   d. pure research.

20. The step in the scientific research cycle that aids in prediction, promotes efficiency, and
    ensures objectivity in the formulation of hypotheses is
    a. the review of literature.   c. analysis of findings.
    b. making observations.   d. reporting results.

Part C: True or False

21. T F A longitudinal study is one that is broad-based and takes place over a brief pe-
           riod of time.

22. T F A biased sample is one that lacks random selection and, in some cases, involves
           self-selection by participants.

23. T F As a science, the most important task of sociology is to develop a constantly ex-
           panding body of reliable knowledge.

24.   T   F   In conducting sociological research, more than one research method—survey, experiment, participant observation, etc.—must never be used in a single study.

25.   T   F   Sociological research has been governed by a well-established code of ethics for over one hundred years.

Test Answers May Be Found on Page 72.

Percentage Score = (Number of items correct × 4) _____.

Chapter 3

Culture: A Way of Life

DESIRED LEARNING OUTCOMES
(A PREVIEW FOR ESS STEP 1)

After successful study of this chapter, the student should be able to

1. define and discuss *culture* as a concept;

2. identify and briefly discuss the chief characteristic that separates human beings from the lower animals in their behavior;

3. discuss the concept of *instinct* as it applies to both lower animals and humans;

4. identify and briefly explain two behaviors that are often confused with instincts;

5. list and briefly discuss the basic characteristics that distinguish human beings from the lower animals;

6. list and briefly discuss the basic characteristics of culture;

7. compare and contrast the concepts of *homogeneous society* and *heterogeneous society;*

8. compare and contrast the concepts of *ethnocentrism, xenophobia,* and *xenocentrism;*

9. show how a *counterculture* is distinguished from a *subculture;*

10. discuss *culture shock;*

11. explain what is meant by *cultural relativity;*

12. define the term *cultural universals* and give at least three examples;

13. explain each of the basic elements of culture: *cognitive culture, normative culture, material culture,* and *language;*

14. trace how the need for social control has been addressed from ancient times to the formation and development of modern societies like the United States;

15. explain what mechanisms of social control are used by cultures and how they operate; and

16. discuss the basic factors that account for how cultures change.

Note: For specific information on how to address the instructions in these DLOs (e. g., "list," "explain," "compare and contrast," etc.), consult pages 107–111 of the ESS supplement that follows this Study Guide.

DEVELOPMENT OF THE COMPREHENSIVE OUTLINE
(USING SKILLS CONTAINED IN ESS STEP 2)

To master the DLOs for Chapter 2, it is recommended that you outline the chapter as explained in ESS. The following is an example of what the "Conformity and Social Order" section of the chapter might look like after you develop your own written outline of it. Since this is the third major heading in the chapter, it is labeled Roman numeral III.

III. Conformity and Social Order
   A. The Need for Social Control (how it has been addressed)
   1. Ancient societies. Example: The Code of Hammurabi developed 4000 years ago in ancient Babyonia (named after the ruler). Consisted of 282 laws covering most social issues.
   2. Rationalistic tradition emerged in the wake of Hammurabi (necessary because promise of otherworldly pleasure or pain in afterlife proved to be ineffective in maintaining conformity in many people).
   3. Social Contract Theories of 1600s and 1700s.
   Social contract—argument that people agreed to give up some freedom (form a social contract) in order to live in peace and harmony.
      a. Thomas Hobbes—seventeenth-century contract theorist. Theory explained in *Leviathan* (1651). Three stages of history: (1) people lived in nature and freely pursued desires, (2) this led to war of "all against all," (3) to effect order, people formed social contract to establish society and government.
      b. John Locke—eighteenth-century contract theorist. Went further than Hobbes in asserting right of revolution for the people if and when their government ceased to address their needs (thus breaking the social contract). Locke's writings influenced Jefferson and formed much of the ideological basis for the American Revolution.
   4. Modern society and needed mechanisms for social control.

    a. Social contract notion not supported by modern behavioral research. Dismissed today as myth.

    b. Instead, research shows that conformity is maintained through basic mechanisms of social control.

B. Mechanisms for Social Control

Social control in any culture maintained through a system of **sanctions**—socially recognized and enforced rewards and punishments.

  1. Characteristics:

    a. may be positive or negative

    b. may be informal or formal

    c. involve a *range of tolerance* before being invoked

  2. Types:

    a. *Positive sanctions*—rewards for obeying norms.

      (1) *Informal positive sanctions*—usually sufficient to maintain conformity (particularly in groups and small communities). Examples: praise, emotional support, affection

      (2) *Formal positive sanctions*—used in school and career settings and in the larger society. Examples: "A" grades, job promotion, civic awards

    b. *Negative sanctions*—punishments for disobeying norms

      (1) *Informal negative sanctions*—usually sufficient. Examples: Criticism, ridicule, "silent treatment"

      (2) *Formal negative sanctions*—usually imposed by organizations and the larger society. Examples: Written reprimand, demotion, dismissal, imprisonment for crime

LEARNING ASSESSMENT TEST
(USING SKILLS CONTAINED IN ESS STEP 3)

Part A: Matching

_e_   **1.** Acculturation

_j_   **2.** Fad

_f_   **3.** Culture

_p_   **4.** Artifacts

_a_   **5.** Instinct

_k_   **6.** Mores

_m_   **7.** Counterculture

_l_   **8.** Knowledge

_b_   **9.** Rules of deference

_g_   **10.** Reflex

a. A genetically determined imperative for complex behavior

b. Folkways that specify how and under what conditions people may show respect for one another

c. A preference for the ways of a foreign culture

d. A disorientation one experiences when placed in a different culture

e. Cultural change brought about by direct contact by two or more cultures

f. A way of life as furnished by a particular society

g. An automatic physical response to an external stimulus by the nervous system

A __ 11. Cultural universals
C __ 12. Xenocentrism
X L __ 13. Cultural lag
X h __ 14. Sapir-Whorf hypothesis
d __ 15. Culture shock

h. The perspective that language structures the way people in particular cultures perceive reality

i. Propositions about reality that can be scientifically supported

j. A folkway popular for only a brief period of time among a limited number of people

k. Norms considered very important so that their violation is sometimes met with severe punishment.

l. The hypothesis that material culture (technology) changes more rapidly than normative culture

m. A type of subculture in basic conflict with the dominant culture of a society

n. Social patterns and practices common to all cultures

o. Rules for carrying out skills or habits associated with technology

p. Physical objects that represent a specific culture

Part B: Multiple Choice

Select the best answer from the choices provided.

16. The tendency to regard one's own culture as superior and others as inferior is termed
    a. xenophobia.
    b. cultural relativity.
    c. xenocentrism.
    d. ethnocentrism.

17. The element of culture that consists of socially agreed-upon standards for thinking, feeling, and acting in society is
    a. cognitive culture.
    b. material culture.
    c. normative culture.
    d. language.

18. Folkways that specify the socially approved ways of presenting oneself in social situations in terms of such things as carriage, dress, and language are
    a. technicways.
    b. rules of demeanor.
    c. rules of deference.
    d. language.

19. The principle that each culture should be seen and understood in its own context apart from a biased comparison with others refer to
    a. xenocentrism.
    b. cultural relativity.
    c. the Sapir-Whorf hypothesis.
    d. the cultural lag hypothesis.

20. The cultural element that consists of the ways in which a culture defines what is real or what exists is
    a. cognitive culture.
    b. material culture.
    c. normative culture.
    d. language.

Part C: True or False

21. (T) F According to available research, humans have no definite instincts.

22. T (F) A heterogeneous society is one whose inhabitants have a similar ethnic heritage.

23. (T) F Culture is the chief characteristic that separates human beings from the lower animals in their behavior.

24. T (F) Laws represent a cognitive element of culture.

25. T (F) Praise, encouragement, and affection represent examples of informal negative sanctions.

Test Answers May Be Found on Page 73.

Percentage Score = (Number of items correct × 4) _____.

Chapter 4

Socialization: The Process of Becoming Human

DESIRED LEARNING OUTCOMES
(A PREVIEW FOR ESS STEP 1)

After successful study of this chapter, the student should be able to

1. define and discuss *socialization* as a concept;

2. briefly explain what is meant by the term *personality;*

3. trace the development of the "nature" argument from its beginning to the present;

4. trace the development of the "nurture" argument from its beginning to the present;

5. discuss the concept of *feral child;*

6. explain what is meant by the term *tabula rasa;*

7. explain the needs served by socialization;

8. discuss the contributions made to socialization theory by each of the following theorists: George Herbert Mead, Charles H. Cooley, and Sigmund Freud;

9. discuss the contributions made to socialization theory by each of the following theorists: Erik Erikson, Jean Piaget, and Lawrence Kohlberg;

10. discuss the impact made on child socialization by each of the following agents of socialization: *family, peer groups,* and *mass media;*

11. demonstrate an understanding of how *anticipatory socialization* impacts on human development both during childhood and later during the adult years;

12. explain the variety of role transitions that may occur during adulthood as a result of *resocialization;*

13. define what is meant by the term *rites of passage* and give at least two examples;

14. discuss the challenges and problems faced by those in the middle years of adulthood; and

15. discuss the challenges and problems faced by the elderly in American society.

DEVELOPMENT OF THE COMPREHENSIVE OUTLINE
(USING SKILLS CONTAINED IN ESS STEP 2)

To master the DLOs for Chapter 4, it is recommended that you outline the chapter as explained in ESS. The following is an example of what the "Needs Served by Socialization" section of the chapter might look like after you develop your own outline of it. Since this is the second major heading in the chapter, it is labeled Roman numeral II.

II. Needs Served by Socialization

    A. Bonding and Emotional Support
        1. Humans require satisfying contact with others. Example: Primate research of Harry Harlow showed that monkeys reared apart from their mothers became extremely maladjusted.
        2. **Bonding**—the process of forming close personal relationships with others. Types: (1) Parent-child, (2) cross-sex, (2) same sex. Parent-child bond most crucial to development of well-adjusted personality. Example: Research by Marshall Klaus et al. on bonding between newborns and their mothers.
    B. Behavioral Boundaries
        1. Socialization teaches persons how to discipline their behavior.
        2. Small children are self-centered, egocentric. Are taught through socialization how to consider needs of others. This is necessary to becoming a well-adjusted adult.
    C. Goal Setting
        Socialization teaches individual how to set meaningful life goals (short-term and long-term) to reinforce disciplined behavior.
    D. Social Survival Skills (coping skills)
        Examples: General ones such as getting along with others, speaking the language, etc.; specialized ones such as occupational and technical skills.

E. Self-Concept
  1. **Self-concept**—the personal assessment people have of their own identity and self-worth and how they fit into the larger community and society.
  2. Elements that make up and contribute to self-concept:
     a. Psychological dimension (how one feels about oneself).
     b. Socialization influences (tend to shape personal assessment).
     c. One's changing social environment (requires adaptation to a variety of influences).

LEARNING ASSESSMENT TEST
(A TEST SIMULATION FOR USE WITH ESS STEP 3)

Part A: Matching

_e_ 1. Rites of passage

_d_ 2. Sensorimotor stage

_l_ 3. Bonding

_i_ 4. Charles H. Cooley

_k_ 5. Sociobiology

_j_ 6. Imitative stage

_m_ 7. Superego

_o_ 8. Peer group

_g_ 9. Resocialization

_a_ 10. Feral child

_h_ 11. Self-concept

_b_ 12. George H. Mead

_n_ 13. Self-fulfilling prophecy

_c_ 14. Socialization

_f_ 15. Youth subculture

a. An alleged child of nature isolated from social contact with others
b. Interactionist who developed the concepts of "I" and "me" related to the self-concept
c. The process through which culture is transmitted and self-concept is formed
d. According to Piaget, the first stage of cognitive development
e. Formal events that signal the end of one status in life and the beginning of another
f. Life-style characteristics and preferences among children and adolescents
g. Abrupt and often fundamental adjustments in adult life-style and life priorities
h. The personal assessment people have of their own identity and self-worth
i. Developer of the "looking-glass self"
j. According to Mead, the first stage of social development
k. The scientific study of the biological basis for behavior
l. The process of forming close relationships with other people
m. According to Freud, the idealized self or conscience
n. A prediction made by a person that something will occur, which is then

"caused" to come true by the person's own actions

o. People of about the same age and social standing

p. A concept developed by Lawrence Kohlberg

Part B: Multiple Choice

Select the best answer from the choices provided.

16. According to George Herbert Mead, the period during middle to late childhood and early adolescence in which the maturing child becomes fully aware of the impersonal sanctions imposed by the larger society is
    a. the imitative stage.
    b. the game stage.
    c. the play stage.
    d. the stage of formal operations.

17. High school or college graduation, getting married, and being promoted in one's job to a new position are most accurately defined as
    a. formal operations.
    b. anticipatory socialization.
    c. the game stage.
    d. rites of passage.

18. Accord to Sigmund Freud, the main control mechanism (governor) in the psyche or personality is
    a. the ego.
    b. the generalized other.
    c. the "I."
    d. the looking-glass self.

19. The theorist regarded as the father of social psychology and one of the founders of symbolic interactionism was
    a. Sigmund Freud.
    b. Jean Piaget.
    c. Erik Erikson.
    d. George Herbert Mead.

20. According to George Herbert Mead, the standards of community behavior expected of anyone placed in a given social position are referred to as
    a. laws.
    b. postconventional morality.
    c. the generalized other.
    d. peer pressure.

Part C: True or False

21. T F The socialization process takes place from birth through the end of adolescence.

22. T F The most advanced and sophisticated level of moral development is conventional morality.

23. T F According to a review of more than 2500 studies, exposure to television violence encourages aggressive behavior in both children and adolescents.

24. (T) F Children isolated from ongoing contact with parents and other caretakers during the first few months and years of life are prone to experience social maladjustment.

25. (T) F According to Charles H. Cooley, our self-image is basically the result of our interactions with others and our interpretations of those interactions.

Test Answers May Be Found on Page 73.

Percentage Score = (Number of items correct × 4) _____.

Chapter 5

Social Organization

DESIRED LEARNING OUTCOMES
(A PREVIEW FOR ESS STEP 1)

After successful study of this chapter, the student should be able to

1. define and discuss *social organization* as a concept;

2. identify and discuss the social needs that serve as the basis for social organization;

3. demonstrate an understanding of *microlevel organization;*

4. demonstrate an understanding of *macrolevel organization;*

5. describe briefly how sociologists may use functionalist, conflict, and interactionist perspectives to study the different levels of social organization;

6. define *means of subsistence* as a concept and briefly explain how it affects macrolevel organization;

7. compare and contrast how at least four different types of societies are organized and give at least one example of each;

8. briefly explain the two basic types of kinship;

9. define what is meant by *fealty* and give at least two examples;

10. identify at least two different types of groups in society;

11. discuss the concept of *social positions* in terms of (a) basic types and (b) the concept of roles (contained within social positions), their importance, and problems associated with them;

12. (a) explain the history of *contract* as a form of social organization and (b) show how it is used today in modern societies at both micro- and macrolevels;

13. explain (a) how *bureaucracy* developed as a form of social organization and (b) why it is important today; and

14. discuss any one or all of the five basic patterns of social interaction.

Note: For specific information on how to address the instructions in these DLOs (e. g., "identify," "explain," "compare and contrast," etc.), consult pages 107–111 of the ESS supplement that follows this Study Guide.

DEVELOPMENT OF THE COMPREHENSIVE OUTLINE
(USING THE SKILLS CONTAINED IN ESS STEP 2)

To master the DLOs in Chapter 5, it is recommended that you outline the chapter as explained in ESS. The following represents an example of what the "Social Needs: The Basis for Organization" section of the chapter might look like after you develop your own outline of it. Since this is the first major heading in the chapter, it is labeled Roman numeral I.

I. Social Needs: The Basis for Organization

The particular form a society takes depends largely on (1) the social needs defined and addressed by society members and (2) the role played by power and conflict in shaping the way this occurs. Basic need categories are about the same in most societies.

    A. Population Maintenance and Control
       1. *Population maintenance*—reproduction of members. Necessary for survival of society. Accomplished by various institutions historically (family, church, etc.) through development of norms that encouraged parenting.
       2. *Population control*—world today is grossly overpopulated. Traditional norms need to change to moderate reproduction; but this remains controversial issue.
    B. *Division of Labor*—allocation of needed tasks to necessary numbers of people.
       1. Traditionally based on sex (man's work, woman's work).
       2. Based on occupation in modern societies today (sexual differences less important today; jobs require technical expertise, not physical labor).
    C. *Communication*—needed to guarantee effective socialization.
       1. Preliterate cultures (spoken language/ oral history only).
       2. Modern societies (written language and mass media).
       3. Issue of access (in totalitarian countries, access controlled by government; in democratic societies, access more open).
    D. Shared Values and Goals: Consensus or Conflict?
       1. *Shared values and goals*—needed for formation of norms and maintenance of order

and societal direction. Example: national goal established by President Kennedy in 1961 to put men on moon by end of decade.

2. Shared values and goals difficult to maintain in changing society with many diverse subcultures and interest groups. Rapid change and social complexity results in **anomie,** a state of confused norms. What constitutes unacceptable behavior is less clear (crime, prejudice, etc. are more prevalent).

3. Conflict perspective—those in positions of political, economic, and social power able to impose their values/ goals on society. Example: Alcohol prohibition in 1920s.

E. The Maintenance of Social Order

To maintain order, every society must have one or more mechanisms of social control (see Chapter 3). Through establishment of norms in basic institutions (family, religion, government, etc.) and application of sanctions for obeying or disobeying them, conformity and order emerge.

1. *Internal social controls*—maintained by the individual as a result of successful socialization (internalized norms).

2. *External social controls*—imposed by society in the form of formal sanctions. Examples: job dismissal, fine, prison.

LEARNING ASSESSMENT TEST
(A TEST SIMULATION FOR USE WITH ESS STEP 3)

Part A: Matching

b 1. Population maintenance

j 2. Contract

f 3. Agrarian societies

i 4. Master status

c 5. External social controls

k 6. Industrial revolution

j 7. Affinial kinship

i 8. Social position

l 9. Role ambiguity

h 10. Bureaucracy

a 11. Exchange

g 12. Information revolution

e 13. Society

a. The idea that people provide assistance to those who have helped them

b. The reproduction of society members

c. Social controls placed on a person's behavior by society

d. A state of confused norms

e. The largest and most complex system of social interaction

f. Societies characterized by advanced farming methods

g. The primary cause of the emergence of postindustrial societies

h. The personal loyalty of a follower to a leader

i. The primary source of a person's social identity

j. A social bond involving the exchange of one promise for another

k. An era that began in England about 1750

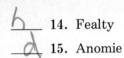 ____ 14. Fealty

____ 15. Anomie

l. Family organization based primarily on marital ties

m. A socially defined location or status a person occupies in society

n. A form of social organization character-ized by professional managers

o. What occurs when obligations that go with a social position are unclear

p. A pattern of social interaction that fos-ters the reduction or resolution of con-flict

Part B: Multiple Choice

Select the best answer from the choices given.

16. A social position assigned to a person at birth or otherwise imposed by society is
    a. an achieved status.
    b. a master status.
    c. an ascribed status.
    d. role strain.

17. The first societies to emerge with the dawn of humankind were
    a. agrarian societies.
    b. hunter-gatherer societies.
    c. pastoral societies.
    d. industrial societies.

18. In the past, most sociologists who studied microlevel organization tended to use the
    a. exchange perspective.
    b. conflict perspective.
    c. interactionist perspective.
    d. functionalist perspective.

19. The type of society that appears to be emerging as a dominant social system for the fu-ture is
    a. the postindustrial society.
    b. the postpastoral society.
    c. the pastoral society.
    d. the agrarian society.

20. The most common form of social interaction is
    a. exchange.
    b. cooperation.
    c. accommodation.
    d. competition.

Part C: True or False

21. T F Most industrial societies today have consanguineal kinship systems.

22. T F Bureaucracy as a form of social organization has been in existence since the building of the pyramids in ancient Egypt.

23. T F By far, the most common form of cooperation, both in past societies and in mod-ern ones today, is spontaneous cooperation or mutual aid.

24. T   F   Macrolevel organization is concerned with the patterned ways in which people
           act at the local community level in social encounters, relationships, and groups.

25. T   F   An ascribed status is a social position earned through individual effort.

Test Answers May Be Found on Page 73.

Percentage Score = (Number of items correct × 4) _____.

Chapter 6

Groups in Society

DESIRED LEARNING OUTCOMES
(A PREVIEW FOR ESS STEP 1)

After successful study of this chapter, the student should be able to

1. define and briefly discuss the concept of *group;*

2. explain the four characteristics that sociologists use to distinguish between the different types of groups; *Common attributes, consciousness of Kind, patterned social relations, formal organization.*

3. compare and contrast the five different types of groups; *Physical aggregate, stat. category, social cat., social group, association*

4. compare and contrast *primary groups* with *secondary groups;*

5. discuss the scope of primary group relations in modern society;

6. discuss the scope of secondary group relations in modern society;

7. briefly explain primary-group versus secondary-group relations in perspective;

8. define and give an example of *polar typology* as a concept;

9. discuss the work of Ferdinand Tönnies as it relates to social organization and the quality of group relations;

10. discuss the work of Émile Durkheim as it relates to social organization and the quality of group relations;

11. define the concept of *group dynamics;*

12. explain at least three basic principles of group dynamics;

13. distinguish between *in-groups* and *out-groups;*

14. discuss what is meant by *social distance;*

15. explain the importance of *reference groups;*

16. explain how the size of *dyads* versus *triads* affects behavior;

17. distinguish between the two basic types of group purpose;

18. compare and contrast *task leaders* with *socioemotional leaders;* and

19. discuss three basic styles of leadership.

Note: For specific information on how to address the instructions in these DLOs (e. g., "identify," "explain," "compare and contrast," etc.), consult pages 107–111 in the ESS supplement that follows this Study Guide.

DEVELOPMENT OF THE COMPREHENSIVE OUTLINE
(USING SKILLS CONTAINED IN ESS STEP 2)

To master the DLOs for Chapter 6, it is recommended that you outline the chapter as explained in ESS. The following is an example of what the "Social Groups" section of the chapter might look like after you develop your own outline of it. Since this is the second major heading of the chapter, it is labeled Roman numeral II.

II. Social Groups

Social group—people bound together by common interests and values in a definite pattern of social interaction. Basic characteristics: common attributes, consciousness of kind, and patterned social relations. Two basic types: primary group and secondary group.

    A. **Primary group**—small group characterized by personalized, ongoing relationships. Examples: family, circle of best friends.
        1. Characteristics:
           a. Relative smallness
           b. Strong affectional ties
           c. Strong personal identification (with group)
           d. Multidimensional relationships
           e. Continuous face-to-face contact
           f. Durability
           g. Based on trust
           h. Informal social controls
        2. The Scope of Primary Relations
           a. Primary relations satisfy our basic needs for emotional intimacy and social sharing. These needs are typically met by the family and circles of close friends.
           b. Informal adaptations—When family and usual friends are not available, the

need to belong and share with others may be met in other ways. Examples: Primary groups formed within military units in wartime; primary groups formed among deviants, such as the "family" bond in juvenile gangs and adult criminal groups and the homosexual "marriages" among inmates in prison.

B. **Secondary group**—relatively large collection of people with whom one has superficial and somewhat impersonal relations. Examples: Relations with most people other than family and close friends.
  1. Characteristics:
     a. Relatively large size
     b. Weak affectional ties
     c. Little or no personal identification
     d. One-dimensional relationships
     e. Limited face-to-face contact
     f. Nonpermanence
     g. Based on distrust
     h. Formal social controls
  2. The Scope of Secondary Relations
     a. In modern urban societies today, most social contacts are secondary rather than primary in nature.
     b. As some sociologists have observed (e. g., Wirth and Simmel), this is necessary given the many specialized roles people must carry out plus the large numbers of people they are surrounded with on a daily basis. Yet, this type of life-style may result not only in indifference toward others but also in some aversion to making contact with most people.

C. Social Group Relations in Perspective
  1. The concepts of *primary group* and *secondary group* indicate ideal types that occupy different ends of a continuum.
  2. In reality, most group relations represent composites. Some are predominantly primary with some secondary elements. Others are predominantly secondary with perhaps a few primary elements to a greater or lesser degree.
  3. The longer we interact with people on a regular basis, the greater the chance that elements of primary relations will emerge.

LEARNING ASSESSMENT TEST
(A TEST SIMULATION FOR USE WITH ESS STEP 3)

Part A: Matching

_____ 1. Authoritarian

_____ 2. Dyad

_____ 3. George Homans

_____ 4. Social category

a. A group used as a standard of comparison to evaluate one's values, behavior, and goals

b. The systematic study of small-group processes

c. A two-person group

___g___   5. The family
___j___   6. Polar typology
___e___   7. Organic solidarity
___b___   8. Group dynamics
___p___   9. Triad
___f___   10. Ferdinand Tönnies
___k___   11. Initiative promotes status
___o___   12. Reference group
___m___   13. Formal organization
___l___   14. Based on distrust
___o___   15. In-group

d. A group a person belongs to or identifies with
e. The solidarity of differences characteristic of modern industrial societies
f. The originator of the *gemeinschaft* versus *gesellschaft* typology
g. A primary group
h. A group whose members have in common one or more visible or otherwise special characteristics
i. A founding father of group dynamics research
j. Two ideal types placed on opposite ends of a continuum
k. A principle of group dynamics
l. A secondary group
m. The action by members of an association to pursue specific practical goals
n. A style of leadership
o. A group a person does not belong to or identify with
p. A three-person group

Part B: Multiple Choice

Select the best answer from the choices given.

16. According to Émile Durkheim, a state of mental and moral agreement among members of a society concerning basic norms and values is
    a. anomie.
    b. consciousness of kind.
    c. the collective conscience.
    d. group dynamics.

17. The degree of acceptance an individual feels toward those who belong to groups to which he or she does not belong is
    a. social distance.
    b. mechanical solidarity.
    c. anomie.
    d. organic solidarity.

18. A society characterized by low levels of technology, slow rates of change, common ancestry among inhabitants, and commonly held norms and values is
    a. *gemeinschaft.*
    b. pastoral.
    c. *gesellschaft.*
    d. postindustrial.

19. A group deliberately formed to pursue one or more specific practical goals is
    a. a physical aggregate.
    b. a social category.
    c. a social group.
    d. an association.

20. A group a person does not belong to or identify with is
   a. a primary group.
   b. an out-group.
   c. an in-group.
   d. a reference group.

Part C: True or False

21. T   F   Taking the initiative in interacting with others discourages friendship.

22. T   F   Social categories typically lack the characteristics of patterned social relations and formal organization.

23. T   F   Members of primary groups typically have one-dimensional relationships with one another.

24. T   F   Mass urban societies today are characterized for the most part by secondary-group relations.

25. T   F   A triad is a two-person group.

Test Answers May Be Found on Page 74.

Percentage Score = (Number of items correct × 4) _____.

Chapter 7

Associations and Bureaucracy

DESIRED LEARNING OUTCOMES
(A PREVIEW FOR ESS STEP 1)

After successful study of this chapter, the student should be able to

1. define *association* as a concept;

2. compare and contrast the different types of associations;

3. discuss *total institutions;*

4. explain the process of *brainwashing;*

5. distinguish between *power* and *authority;*

6. discuss the different types of power;

7. discuss Weber's historical analysis of authority;

8. explain what is meant by the *iron law of oligarchy;*

9. demonstrate an understanding of Weber's bureaucratic model;

10. explain the extent to which individuals may succumb to group pressure and conform in organizational work settings;

11. explain *groupthink* in terms of how it may impact on conformity in associations;

12. discuss the *collective* as an alternative to bureaucratic organization;

13. discuss the Japanese corporation as an alternative to bureaucracy in Western societies;

14. explain how the association is structured as a total social system; and

15. identify and discuss at least three problems that plague some large-scale associations.

Note: For specific information on how to address the instructions in these DLOs (e. g., "discuss," "explain," "compare and contrast," etc.), consult pages 107–111 of the ESS supplement that follows this Study Guide.

DEVELOPING THE COMPREHENSIVE OUTLINE
(USING SKILLS CONTAINED IN ESS STEP 2)

To master the DLOs for Chapter 7, it is recommended that you outline the chapter as explained in ESS. The following is an example of what the "Problems of Large-Scale Associations" section of the chapter might look like after you develop your own written outline of it. Since this is the fifth major heading in the chapter, it is labeled Roman numeral V.

V. Problems of Large-Scale Associations

A. **Ritualism**—overconformity to the rules of the organization by an individual participant. Example: An inflexible bureaucrat tied to the letter rather than the spirit of "company policy," although the client and the goals of the organization itself are poorly served.

B. **Goal displacement**—a situation in which the means (rules) of an organization become substituted for the goals and participants lose sight of their original objective. Example: A school system that spends an inappropriate amount of its budget on administration as compared with instruction.

C. **Protection of incompetence**—a problem that occurs when an organization fails first to identify and then develop, reassign, or remove inadequate performers. Example: The practice by some participants in organizations of protecting fellow employees who are poor performers.

D. The **Peter principle**—the tendency for officials to keep rising within an organization until they eventually reach their levels of incompetence. Example: The employee promoted to management through seniority who, because of a lack of aptitude, training, or both, is incapable of doing an adequate job.

E. **Parkinson's law**—a problem in organizations in which "work expands to fill the time available for its completion." Example: The employee who appears busy but does not have enough work to justify his or her position.

LEARNING ASSESSMENT TEST
(A TEST SIMULATION FOR USE WITH ESS STEP 3)

Part A: Matching

_____ 1. Written rules

_____ 2. Groupthink

_____ 3. Total institution

_____ 4. A king or queen

_____ 5. Max Weber

_____ 6. The collective

_____ 7. Personalized work setting

_____ 8. Task leadership

_____ 9. Ritualism

_____ 10. Formal structure

_____ 11. Degradation rituals

_____ 12. Robert Michels

_____ 13. Referent power

_____ 14. A physician

_____ 15. Lifetime employment

a. A part of the organizational climate the informal structure helps to promote
b. A requirement for effective management of the formal structure of a large-scale association
c. A characteristic of Weber's bureaucratic model
d. One who possesses traditional authority
e. A characteristic of many Japanese corporations
f. An extreme form of coercive association
g. The author of the iron law of oligarchy
h. An alternative to bureaucratic organization
i. One who possesses rational-legal authority
j. Procedures and activities designed to disorient emotionally the new members of a total institution
k. The ability of a person to attract personally or appeal to others
l. Overconformity to the rules of an organization
m. The author of _Economy and Society_ who developed a typology of three forms of legitimate authority
n. The official goals, policies, and procedures of an association
o. The result when group decisions are made uncritically with little or no conflict for the sake of cohesion and "good relations"
p. One who possesses charismatic authority

Part B: Multiple Choice

Select the best answer from the choices provided.

16. The ability to influence or control the behavior of others with or without their consent is
    a. ritualism.
    b. authority.
    c. power.
    d. groupthink.

17. Small businesses and volunteer groups that function on nonbureaucratic principles are
    a. collectives.
    b. utilitarian associations.
    c. coercive associations.
    d. Japanese corporations.

18. Those whom others believe are more knowledgeable than they are in a certain area of expertise tend to possess
    a. reward power.
    b. referent power.
    c. coercive power.
    d. expert power.

19. A form of authority based on the belief by followers that the leader possesses special qualities or unique personal characteristics is
    a. charismatic authority.
    b. rational-legal authority.
    c. traditional authority.
    d. utilitarian authority.

20. The company for which one is employed full-time is an example of
    a. a traditional association.
    b. a utilitarian association.
    c. a voluntary association.
    d. a coercive association.

Part C: True or False

21. T F Prisons, mental institutions, and prisoner of war camps are representative examples of utilitarian associations.

22. T F According to Robert Michels, the principle that power in organizations invariably becomes concentrated in the hands of a few people is the iron law of oligarchy.

23. T F Legitimate power is called *authority*.

24. T F The protection of incompetence occurs when an organization fails first to identify and then develop, reassign, or remove inadequate performers.

25. T F Weber's bureaucratic model represents a model of the informal structure of large-scale associations.

Test Answers May Be Found on Page 74.

Percentage Score = (Number of items correct × 4) _____.

Chapter 8

Social Stratification

DESIRED LEARNING OUTCOMES
(A PREVIEW FOR ESS STEP 1)

After successful study of this chapter, the student should be able to

1. define *social stratification* as a concept;

2. discuss differential *life chances* in the United States;

3. explain the various ways in which sociologists define and assess poverty;

4. describe the poor in America;

5. explain what is meant by the *culture of poverty hypothesis;*

6. explain what is meant by *structural unemployment;*

7. list and discuss at least three myths about welfare and the poor in America;

8. compare and contrast the functionalist, conflict, and evolutionary perspectives used by sociologists to explain stratification;

9. discuss the different types of stratification systems;

10. distinguish between *power elite theory* and *pluralistic theory;*

11. list and discuss the most important indicators of prestige in America;

12. explain how wealth is acquired and concentrated in America;

13. discuss life-style as an element of stratification;

14. explain the subjective approach to stratification analysis;

15. explain the reputational approach to stratification analysis; and

16. explain the objective approach to stratification analysis.

Note: For specific information on how to address the instructions in these DLOs (e. g., "list," "explain," "compare and contrast," etc.), consult pages 107–111 of the ESS supplement that follows this Study Guide.

DEVELOPMENT OF THE COMPREHENSIVE OUTLINE
(USING SKILLS CONTAINED IN ESS STEP 2)

To master the DLOs for Chapter 8, it is recommended that you outline the chapter as explained in ESS. The following is an example of what the "Analysis of Stratification" section of the chapter might look like after you develop your own outline of it. Since this is the fifth major heading in the chapter, it is labeled Roman numeral V.

V. The Analysis of Stratification

Sociologists use a variety of research approaches to analyze stratification.

- A. The **subjective approach**—a method of analysis in which people are asked to rank themselves.
  1. Benefit: Furnishes sociologists with a means of comparing perceived social rank with actual placement on the stratification scale.
  2. Findings: Most Americans perceive themselves as middle class, regardless of actual socioeconomic position.
- B. The **reputational approach**—a method of analysis in which people are asked to identify the social class of others in their community.
  1. Benefit: Useful for study of rank in local communities.
  2. Findings: There are usually five to six distinct class levels in most American communities
  3. Pioneering research: W. Lloyd Warner's "Yankee City" study. Warner found six classes:
     a. *Upper-upper class*—old, established upper-class families; three or more generations of prominence.
     b. *Lower-upper class*—those with newly acquired wealth and social standing; "new money."
     c. *Upper-middle class*—college-educated professionals and successful businesspeople; property owners; substantial income.
     d. *Lower-middle class*—lower-level white-collar workers and skilled blue-collar workers; live in small houses in neat neighborhoods.
     e. *Upper-lower class*—semiskilled and unskilled blue-collar workers; "poor but honest" reputation.

    f. *Lower-lower class*—the underemployed and unemployed; seen in commuity as lazy, dependent.

C. The **objective approach**—a method of analysis that makes use of standardized criteria for measuring social rank.

    1. Benefit: Use of standardized criteria (e. g., occupation, education, etc.); more useful as applied to large populations.

    2. Most common application: *Socioeconomic status* (SES), composite ranking that uses occupation, education, and income.

LEARNING ASSESSMENT TEST
(A TEST SIMULATION FOR USE WITH ESS STEP 3)

Part A: Matching

_____ 1. Socioecnomic status (SES)

_____ 2. Life chances

_____ 3. Apartheid

_____ 4. Horizontal mobility

_____ 5. Wealth

_____ 6. Estate system

_____ 7. Relative poverty

_____ 8. W. Lloyd Warner

_____ 9. Subjective approach

_____ 10. Lower-upper class

_____ 11. Meritocracy

_____ 12. Caste system

_____ 13. Prestige

_____ 14. Oscar Lewis

_____ 15. Vertial mobility

a. A system of rigid racial segregation (caste) in South Africa

b. Those with newly acquired wealth and social standing

c. Developed the culture of poverty hypothesis

d. The perspective that society is dominated by the most talented who deserve most of the rewards

e. An objective approach at assessing social rank

f. Change in social position (such as occupation) with no change in social class level

g. Pioneered the reputational approach to stratification analysis

h. Opportunities for survival and prosperity in society

i. A person's net worth in property and income

j. Any upward or downward change in one's social class level

k. A system of stratification based on family membership and landholdings

l. A method of stratification study in which people rank themselves

m. A standard of living that is substandard compared to that of most members of society

n. The relative degree of honor and respect received from others

o. The lack of essential resources needed for survival

p. A rigid system of stratification in which social position is inherited and remains the same for life

Part B: Multiple Choice

Select the best answer from the choices provided.

16. The most important source of prestige in the United States is
    a. occupation.
    b. wealth.
    c. education.
    d. social visibility.

17. The perspective that poverty involves a subculture that socializes its children to accept being poor as natural and normal for them is
    a. apartheid.
    b. the culture of poverty hypothesis.
    c. power-elite theory.
    d. the conflict perspective.

18. A contradiction that occurs when a person seems to rank higher on one aspect of stratification than another is
    a. anomie.
    b. relative deprivation.
    c. structural unemployment.
    d. status inconsistency.

19. The perspective that stratification is necessary and beneficial because it provides a system of rewards that motivates people to seek and fill the most valued positions is the
    a. conflict perspective.
    b. estate perspective.
    c. evolutionary perspective.
    d. functionalist perspective.

20. A person's general value orientation, tastes and preferences, and pattern of living refers to
    a. life chances.
    b. prestige.
    c. life-style.
    d. power.

Part C: True or False

21. T F The loss of employment as a result of economic changes that render certain occupations obsolete is structural unemployment.

22. T F *Felt poverty* is an official designation as determined by an agreed-upon standard, such as annual income.

23. T F The higher one's social class, the shorter one's life expectancy tends to be.

24. T F Dramatic life-style differences exist between those in the upper class versus those who occupy the upper-lower or working class.

25.   T   F   The majority of poor families receiving public assistance (Aid to Families with Dependent Children) have only one or two children.

Test Answers May Be Found on Page 74.

Percentage Score = (Number of items correct × 4) _____.

Chapter 9

Racial and Ethnic Minorities

DESIRED LEARNING OUTCOMES
(A PREVIEW FOR ESS STEP 1)

After successful study of this chapter, the student should be able to

1. compare and contrast the concepts *majority group* and *minority group;*

2. list and explain the basic characteristics of minority groups;

3. distinguish between the two basic types of minorities;

4. discuss the basic types of prejudice;

5. define and briefly discuss the concept of *stereotypes;*

6. identify the basic difference between *prejudice* and *discrimination;*

7. discuss the basic types of discrimination;

8. explain how prejudice and discrimination relate to each other;

9. discuss *race* both as a biological concept and a sociological concept;

10. explain the nature of *racism* in terms of definition, origins and history in America, and types;

11. discuss each of the following racial minorities in America: black Americans, Native Americans, and Asian Americans;

12. briefly explain the nature of *ethnicity;*

13. discuss Hispanics as an ethnic minority category;

14. discuss white ethnics as an ethnic minority category;

15. identify and briefly explain three basic types of exclusion that have been experienced by minorities; and

16. identify and briefly explain three basic types of participation experienced by minorities in the larger society.

Note: For specific information on how to address the instructions in these DLOs (e. g., "list," "explain," "compare and contrast," etc.), consult pages 107–111 of the ESS supplement that follows this Study Guide.

DEVELOPMENT OF THE COMPREHENSIVE OUTLINE
(USING SKILLS CONTAINED IN ESS STEP 2)

To master the DLOs for Chapter 9, it is recommended that you outline your chapter as explained in ESS. The following is an example of what the "Prejudice and Discrimination" section of the chapter might look like after you develop your own outline of it. Since this is the second major heading in the chapter, it is labeled Roman numeral II.

II. Prejudice and Discrimination

    A. The Nature of Prejudice
        1. Definitions (general and specific):
            a. Prejudice—the judgment of anything on the basis of preconceived ideas.
            b. **Prejudice**—the negative judgment of individuals and groups because of preconceived ideas held about them.
        2. Types:
            a. **Exploitative prejudice**—negative attitudes toward minority group members held by a majority group, which serve as justification for keeping them in a subordinate position. Example: forcing Indians off their lands in nineteenth century, using as justification the assertion that they were only "heathen savages."
            b. **Normative prejudice**—negative attitudes toward members of a particular group, which are accepted as normal through the process of socialization. Example: Attitudes that blacks and whites should be separate, women belong in the home, etc.
            c. **Authoritarian personality**—a highly rigid and intolerant person who tends to possess a group of identifiable personality characteristics. Examples of typical characteristics:

(1) Sees reality in simplistic dichotomies of good/ bad, us/ them, right/ wrong, etc.

(2) Submissive to those above them in authority, punitive to those below them in authority.

3. **Stereotypes**—fixed mental images about the characteristics of entire categories of people, which are not tested against reality. Examples: Mexicans are lazy, athletes are dumb, etc.

B. The Nature of Discrimination

1. Whereas prejudice is an attitude, **discrimination** refers to differential treatment of people based on their membership in a particular social category.

2. Types:

a. **Individual discrmination**—results when individuals belonging to one group treat members of another group differently because of their group membership. Example: Individual employer who won't hire people over forty.

b. **Institutional discrimination**—involves the unequal treatment of certain categories of people that occurs when inequities are built into basic institutions. Example: Blacks and American Indians denied the right to vote until the 1860s and 1920s, respectively.

c. **Reverse discrmination**—unfair treatment of individuals because they belong to the dominant or majority group. Example: Abuses of *affirmative action* programs (designed to promote equal opportunity) in which minority applicants are hired largely or solely because of minority membership.

C. The Relationship Between Prejudice and Discrmination. (The two sometimes appear together, sometimes not.)

1. *Unprejudiced nondiscrimination* (by "all-weather liberals")
2. *Unprejudiced discrimination* (by "fair-weather liberals")
3. *Prejudiced nondiscrimination* (by "fair-weather bigots")
4. *Prejudiced discrimination* (by "all-weather bigots")

LEARNING ASSESSMENT TEST
(A TEST SIMULATION FOR USE WITH ESS 3)

Part A: Matching

_____ 1. Minority group

_____ 2. Racial minority

_____ 3. Black Americans

_____ 4. Assimilation

_____ 5. Stereotypes

_____ 6. Ethnicity

_____ 7. Jewish Americans

a. Many in this group came to the United States to escape Nazism

b. Fixed mental images about entire categories of people not tested against reality

c. A group of people distinguished by physical or cultural characteristics whose members are not given equal treatment within a society

d. A practice engaged in by "fair-weather liberals"

_____ 8. Majority group

_____ 9. *De jure* segregation

_____ 10. Asian Americans

_____ 11. Prejudiced discrimination

_____ 12. American Indians

_____ 13. Unprejudiced discrimination

_____ 14. Genocide

_____ 15. Ethnic minority

e. The largest racial minority in the United States

f. A practice engaged in by "all-weather bigots"

g. The process of a minority's changing its cultural patterns to adapt to the ways of the dominant culture

h. The most extreme form of exclusion

i. A group that suffers social disadvantages because of visible physical characteristics

j. A minority overrepresented each fall among students in leading American universities

k. The dominant group in terms of power, prestige, wealth, and culture

l. A group that experiences social disadvantages because of its cultural characteristics

m. The intermarriage of minority group members with members of the majority group

n. Segregation by law

o. The specific cultural heritage that distinguishes one group from another

p. The poorest American minority

Part B: Multiple Choice

Select the best answer from the choices provided.

16. Statutes enacted during the late nineteenth century that denied blacks free access to public facilities used by whites such as restaurants, rail cars, and restrooms were
    a. acts of *de facto* segregation.
    b. acts of normative prejudice.
    c. acts of reverse discrimination.
    d. Jim Crow laws.

17. Members of an Asian minority incarcerated in American detention camps during World War II were
    a. Japanese Americans.
    b. Korean Americans.
    c. Chinese Americans.
    d. Vietnamese Americans.

18. Statements such as "Jews are stingy," "Athletes are dumb," and "Mexicans are lazy" represent examples of
    a. segregation.
    b. institutional discrimination.
    c. stereotypes.
    d. accommodation.

19. A fast-growing minority that, if current trends continue, could outnumber blacks by early in the twenty-first century are
    a. Asian Americans.   c. American Indians.
    b. Hispanics.   d. Jewish Americans.

20. The intentional and systematic attempt by one group to exterminate another is referred to as
    a. amalgamation.   c. segregation.
    b. genocide.   d. normative prejudice.

Part C: True or False

21. T F Of all Hispanics, Mexican Americans are closest to the American mainstream in annual family income and life chances.

22. T F *Pan-Indianism* refers to attempts by several Indian groups to develop coalitions between tribes to face common problems.

23. T F Whereas prejudice is an attitude, discrimination refers to differential treatment of people based on their membership in a particular social category.

24. T F Members of minority groups lack a consciousness of kind or sense of peoplehood.

25. T F The concept of race as a "pure type" is regarded as a social myth by sociologists and is of little value to science.

Test Answers May Be Found on Page 74.

Percentage Score = (Number of items correct × 4) _____.

Chapter 10

Collective Behavior

DESIRED LEARNING OUTCOMES
(A PREVIEW FOR ESS STEP 1)

After successful study of this chapter, the student should be able to

1. define and briefly discuss *collective behavior* as a concept;

2. define what is meant by *value-added theory;*

3. discuss *structural conduciveness;*

4. explain the two basic sources of *structural strain;*

5. define and give an example of *generalized belief;*

6. discuss *precipitating factors* as they relate to collective behavior;

7. discuss *mobilization of participants* as a factor relating to collective behavior;

8. explain how agents of social control may affect the direction and extent of collective behavior;

9. discuss the nature of crowds in terms of at least two of their characteristics;

10. discuss Herbert Blumer's typology of crowds;

11. compare and contrast at least two different explanations of crowd behavior;

12. define and briefly explain what is meant by *mass behavior;*

13. define and briefly explain the concepts of *fads, crazes,* and *fashions;*

14. discuss *rumors* as a form of mass behavior;

15. discuss *urban legends* as a form of mass behavior;

16. explain what is meant by *mass hysteria;*

17. discuss the concept of *public;*

18. discuss *public opinion* and the factors affecting it;

19. demonstrate an understanding of *propaganda;* and

20. discuss *social movements.*

Note: For specific information on how to address the instructions in these DLOs (e. g., "list," "explain," "compare and contrast," etc.), consult pages 107–111 of the ESS supplement that follows this Study Guide.

DEVELOPMENT OF THE COMPREHENSIVE OUTLINE
(USING SKILLS CONTAINED IN ESS STEP 2)

To master the DLOs for Chapter 10, it is recommended that you outline the chapter as explained in ESS. The following is an example of what the "Mass Behavior" section of the chapter might look like after you develop your own comprehensive outline of it. Since this the fourth major heading in the chapter, it is labeled Roman numeral IV.

IV. Mass Behavior

Mass behavior—unstructured social behavior characteristic of large collectivities of people who operate outside each other's presence.

    A. Fads, Crazes, and Fashions
        Variations of folkways (see Chapter 3) that are also forms of collective behavior.
        1. *Fads*—folkways popular for brief periods of time within a limited segment of the population. Examples: Fad diets, music, slang expressions.
        2. *Crazes*—fads that become obsessive within a limited segment of society. Examples: "Pet rocks" in 1970s, obsession with cult personalities like athletes, musical entertainers, etc.
        3. *Fashions*—folkways more durable than fads, which gain widespread acceptance for a substantial period of time. Examples: Certain clothing styles, driving smaller cars than in decades past, small families, not smoking.
    B. Rumors
        1. Definition: **Rumor**—an unconfirmed story that is spread rather quickly from person to person. Examples: Beatle (at that time) Paul McCartney is dead (1969); Proctor & Gamble logo is satanic symbol (1970s–1985).
        2. Reason for spread of rumors: They act as substitute for news, particularly in times of social strain and confusion.
        3. Rumors can be destructive: Have touched off panic and riots, destroyed reputations, etc.

   4. How rumors spread: Four factors (often occur in sequence)
      a. *Leveling*—a process in which, as the rumor is told and retold, it becomes more concise with fewer details.
      b. *Sharpening*—a process in which details that are retained increase in importance and become the main story.
      c. *Correcting*—a process in which people make changes in an already distorted rumor so that details (often out of context due to sharpening) will fit together "logically."
      d. *Exaggeration*—the addition of new details that can make an interesting story even more exciting.
   C. Urban Legends
      1. **Urban legend**—an unsubstantiated story much more durable than a rumor, which is spread over an entire country, usually with several local variations. Examples: Dog in the microwave, death of "little Mikey," "killer in the back seat."
      2. Contain themes consistent with issues of modern life.
      3. A rumor tends to become urban legend when it (a) is a good story, (b) seems plausible, (c) offers a moral object lesson.
      4. Popular themes: Restroom legends, stories of "suppressed truth," unfortunate pets, sex scandals, unusual revenge.
   D. Mass Hysteria
      1. **Mass hysteria**—a spontaneous fearful reaction by large numbers of people to a mysterious social condition or event perceived as a threat. Examples: Panic resulting from collapse of stock market in 1929, the "Red scare" in the early 1950s instigated by Joseph McCarthy.
      2. May occur at both microlevel (community) and macrolevel (society).

LEARNING ASSESSMENT TEST
(A TEST SIMULATION FOR USE WITH ESS STEP 3)

Part A: Matching

_____ 1. Convergence theory	a. Developed emergent norm theory
_____ 2. Neil Smelser	b. Limitations placed on information that is made available to the public
_____ 3. Imitation	c. Attempt to work within the social system for change in policy, etc.
_____ 4. Collective behavior	d. One explanation of crowd behavior
_____ 5. Rumor	e. A condition in which a person's identity becomes lost in a crowd
_____ 6. Mass behavior	f. Originated social contagion theory
_____ 7. Structural strain	g. Relatively spontaneous and unstructured actions of people in response to ambiguous or changing conditions
_____ 8. Reform movements	
_____ 9. Gustave Le Bon	h. Fads that have become obsessive

_____ 10. Bystander apathy

_____ 11. Crazes

_____ 12. Mob

_____ 13. Censorship

_____ 14. Anonymity

_____ 15. Social unrest stage

i. The beginning period of a social movement

j. One principal cause of social contagion

k. An unconfirmed story

l. A component of value-added theory

m. A category of collective behavior that includes fads, rumors, and urban legends

n. A term applied to the condition of onlookers in a crowd who fail to act in a situation of emergency

o. The most extreme form of acting crowd

p. Developed value-added theory

Part B: Multiple Choice

Select the best answer from the choices provided.

16. An emergent popular explanation of both the causes and solutions to a perceived social problem (a component of value-added theory) is
    a. structural conduciveness.
    b. generalized belief.
    c. structural strain.
    d. social control.

17. According to Herbert Blumer, a fairly structured crowd that conforms to established norms is
    a. a casual crowd.
    b. an expressive crowd.
    c. a conventional crowd
    d. an acting crowd.

18. An attempt to replace all or a portion of the existing social system with something different, through violent means if necessary, describes the approach taken by
    a. separatist movements.
    b. conservative movements.
    c. reform movements.
    d. revolutionary movements.

19. The argument that certain social conditions, when added together, create a cumulative effect and increase the likelihood of collective behavior refers to
    a. value-added theory.
    b. convergence theory.
    c. emergent norm theory.
    d. social contagion theory.

20. An unsubstantiated story, much longer-lasting than a rumor, that is spread throughout the country is called
    a. a craze.
    b. an urban legend.
    c. circular reaction.
    d. suggestibility.

Part C: True or False

21. T F *Sharpening* refers to a process in which, as a rumor is circulated and certain details are lost, those that remain increase in importance and become the main story.

22. T F Mass behavior represents one of the most durable and structured forms of collective behavior.

23. T F Like brainwashing, the primary purpose of propaganda is to "reprogram" an individual or group with a different set of basic values.

24. T F Characteristics of social movements include idealism among members, an action orientation, and multiple organizations.

25. T F Rumors tend to emerge from conditions of social strain and confusion in which there is an unsatisfied demand for news.

Test Answers May Be Found on Page 74.

Percentage Score = (Number of items correct × 4) _____.

Chapter 11

Deviant Behavior

DESIRED LEARNING OUTCOMES
(A PREVIEW FOR USE WITH ESS STEP 1)

After successful study of this chapter, the student should be able to

1. compare and contrast the concepts *deviance* and *deviant;*

2. discuss deviance as a social definition;

3. list and briefly explain some social benefits that may derive from deviance;

4. list and briefly explain some negative effects of deviance;

5. briefly explain why it is important to understand conformity in order to analyze deviant behavior;

6. discuss the two basic types of conformity;

7. demonstrate an understanding of how conformity is maintained;

8. list and briefly discuss the different levels of deviance in society;

9. list and explain the basic types of deviance;

10. discuss *demonology* and *astrology* as early explanations of deviance;

11. (a) identify when the first scientific explanations of deviance emerged and (b) define the nature of their focus;

12. trace the history of the biological explanations of deviance and place them in perspective;

13. argue in detail how deviance might be explained using the functionalist approach;

14. argue in detail how deviance might be explained using the conflict approach;

15. argue in detail how deviance might be explained using the interactionist approach; and

16. place in perspective the three basic sociological approaches used to analyze deviance.

Note: For specific information on how to address the instructions in these DLOs (e. g., "list," "trace," "explain," etc.), consult pages 107–111 of the ESS supplement that follows this Study Guide.

DEVELOPMENT OF THE COMPREHENSIVE OUTLINE
(USING THE SKILLS CONTAINED IN ESS STEP 2)

To master the DLOs for Chapter 11, it is recommended that you outline the chapter as explained in ESS. The following is an example of what "The Nature of Deviance" section of the chapter might look like after you develop your own outline of it. Since this is the first major heading in the chapter, it is labeled Roman numeral I.

I. The Nature of Deviance

    A. Deviance and Deviants

        1. **Deviance**—behavior that violates the dominant norms of a group or society. Origin of dominant norms: Those with power have their standards for behavior instituted as social policy. How behavioral standards are acquired: Through socialization, we learn what is considered legal, moral, "normal," etc. Who engages in deviance: Practically everyone engages in minor forms of deviance.

        2. **Deviant**—a person who violates the most highly regarded norms of a group or society. Examples: Delinquents, criminals, prostitutes. Response by society: The deviant is rejected as a person of value by most; in many cases, severe punishment results.

    B. Deviance as a Social Definition

    What is considered unacceptable behavior varies according to several factors:

        1. *Deviance and one's social context.* What is legal, moral, and acceptable varies from society to society.

        2. *Deviance and one's position in society.* Examples: Childern cannot vote, felons cannot legally buy handguns.

        3. *Deviance and historical time frame.* Example: Prior to 1973, abortion was illegal in U. S.

    C. Social Benefits That Derive from Deviance

    Sometimes deviance may have some positive consequences:

        1. *Deviance may increase group cohesion.* Example: Crime wave may result in restored community cohesion.

2. *Deviance may help to clarify social norms.* Example: Laws perceived as out-of-date may be tested in the courts.
3. *Toleration of some deviance may help minimize more severe forms.* Examples: Use of minor criminals as informants by police.
4. *Deviance may help bring about changes in social policy.* Examples: Nonviolent civil disobedience in 1960s helped to bring about key civil rights legislation.

D. Negative Effects of Deviance
Deviance often causes social disruption and serious problems:
1. *Deviance disrupts social order.* Example: High crime rates reduce safety and increase social and financial costs.
2. *Deviance destroys motivaton of others to conform.* Example: The money to be made selling illegal drugs.
3. *Deviance undermines trust in organizations and institutions.* Example: Sex scandals involving ministers; scandals involving the highest levels of government.
4. *Deviance is expensive.* Example: The billions of dollars in losses from shoplifting passed on to consumers in higher costs for services and merchandise.

LEARNING ASSESSMENT TEST
(A TEST SIMULATION FOR USE WITH ESS STEP 3)

Part A: Matching

_H_ 1. Deviance

_M_ 2. Sanctions

_G_ 3. Aberrant deviance

_P_ 4. Astrology

_K_ 5. Cesare Lombroso

_D_ 6. Retreatism

_C_ 7. Deviant

_D_ 8. Differential association

_B_ 9. William Sheldon

_I_ 10. Conformity

_L_ 11. Argot

_K_ 12. Robert Merton

_J_ 13. Secondary deviance

_A_ 14. Biological explanations

_C_ 15. Group-level deviance

a. The first attempts made to explain deviance from a scientific perspective
b. The originator of somotype theory
c. One who violates the most highly regarded norms of society
d. One who obeys the most important norms of society
e. Activities by a juvenile gang or prostitution ring
f. The developer of anomie theory
g. A form of deviance in which a person violates a norm for selfish reasons and attempts to escape detection and punishment
h. Behavior in basic agreement with the dominant norms of society
i. Behavior that violates the dominant norms of a group or society
j. From a labeling perspective, deviant behavior that is ongoing and habitual
k. The developer of atavistic theory
l. A special form of language characteristic of subcultures

m. Socially recognized and enforced re-wards and punishments
n. The principle that criminal behavior is learned in close-knit groups that con-done or encourage deviant behavior
o. A deviant response in which a person re-jects both culturally approved means and goals
p. The belief that the movement of the planets and stars affects human behav-ior, including deviance

Part B: Multiple Choice

16. Socially disapproved behavior in which a person challenges the legitimacy of certain norms by violating them openly is
    a. aberrant deviance.
    b. nonconforming deviance.
    c. group-level deviance.
    d. socially acceptable deviance.

17. The perspective that deviance results from discrepancies between culturally approved goals and access to the culturally approved means to achieve them is
    a. anomie theory.
    b. differential association.
    c. cultural transmisson theory.
    d. XYY theory.

18. A system of beliefs which holds that deviant behavior is caused by evil spirits that pos-sess the body and make it act according to their will is
    a. cultural transmision theory.
    b. astrology.
    c. demonology.
    d. differential association.

19. Which of the following represents a sociological explanation of deviance that reflects the functionalist perspective?
    a. Labeling theory.
    b. Anomie theory.
    c. Differential association.
    d. None of the above.

20. A deviant response in which a person rejects both culturally approved means and goals, and seeks to replace them with other goals and means is
    a. innovation.
    b. retreatism.
    c. ritualism.
    d. rebellion.

Part C: True or False

21. T F Aberrant deviance refers to a process in which those with certain physical or so-cial characteristics—such as dwarfs, the mentally retarded, and transsexuals—are often perceived and treated as deviant.

22. T F Under certain circumstances, deviance may help to bring about changes in so-cial policy.

23. (T) F Cultural transmission theory asserts that socialization experiences within certain groups encourage the individual to engage in deviant behavior.

24. (T) F According to Edwin Lemert, an early labeling theorist, primary deviance takes the form of impulsive episodes of socially acceptable behavior that are temporary rather than habitual.

25. T (F) The father of the biological school of deviance was William Sheldon, an Italian psychiatrist.

Test Answers May Be Found on Page 75.

Percentage Score = (Number of items correct × 4) _____.

Chapter 12

Population: An Overcrowded Planet

DESIRED LEARNING OUTCOMES
(A PREVIEW FOR USE WITH ESS STEP 1)

After successful study of this chapter, the student should be able to

1. define and briefly discuss *population* as a concept;

2. briefly explain what *demography* represents;

3. discuss sources that demographers use to gather data on populations;

4. explain the theory of *demographic transition;*

5. explain *Malthusian theory;*

6. discuss from a historical perspective how technology has affected world population growth;

7. list and define the chief factors that account for population change;

8. discuss *fertility* as a factor affecting population change;

9. discuss *mortality* as a factor affecting population change;

10. discuss *migration* as a factor affecting population change;

11. define and briefly explain the following concepts as they relate to population change: *age composition, sex composition,* and *population pyramids;*

12. explain the whys of the world "population explosion";

13. discuss the implications for *human ecology* brought about by world population growth;

14. explain what China has done to bring its population under control; and

15. discuss some solutions needed to achieve world population stability.

Note: For specific information on how to address the instructions in these DLOs (e. g., "identify," "discuss," "explain," etc.), consult pages 107–111 of the ESS supplement that follows this Study Guide.

DEVELOPMENT OF THE COMPREHENSIVE OUTLINE
(USING SKILLS CONTAINED IN ESS STEP 2)

To master the DLO's for Chapter 12, it is recommended that you outline the chapter as explained in ESS. The following is an example of what "The Population Dilemma" section of the chapter might look like after you develop your own outline of it. Since this is the fourth major heading in the chapter, it is labeled Roman numeral IV.

IV. The Population Dilemma
  A. The Whys of the "Population Explosion"
       1. **Mortality intervention**—the provision of medical and health technology and assistance to less developed countries by developed nations. Example: The United States has provided many billions of dollars in foreign aid to less developed countries, the greater part since the end of World War II. Effect: Mortality has been drastically reduced in these countries, and rates of population increase have doubled.
       2. **Pronatalism**—a cultural orientation that strongly encourages childbearing. This was necessary in the past, given high rates of mortality and an agricultural economic system that benefited from child labor. Conditions have changed; nonetheless, the pronatalist orientation continues in some countries.
       3. **Lack of Contraception**—in some countries, many people do not know about birth control (little education), nor are contraceptives available to them. Therefore, while mortality rates approach those of developed nations, birth rates remain twice as high. Effect: Population explosion.
  B. Implications for Human Ecology
       1. Definition: **Human ecology**—the scientific study of the relationship between human populations and their natural environments.
          Findings: If current trends of overpopulation are not reversed soon, a severe ecological crisis may occur.
       2. Implications:

   a. **Food**—Many countries (Bolivia, Chile, Pakistan, Peru, etc.) are unable to generate enough calories per person to sustain life; the situation is getting worse.

   b. **Land Resources**—Example: Permanent depletion of the world's rain forests—50,000 acres daily; result is irreversible desert as the result of tropical rains that erode soil because there are no roots to hold soil nutrients.

   c. **Pollution**—Accelerating industrialization produces poisonous wastes faster than environment can absorb them. Example: **Greenhouse effect**—condition of increasing cloud cover caused by air pollution which retains warmth of sun causing higher temperatures.

   d. **Energy**—Growing populations and industrialization produce increasing demands for energy. Since the planet Earth has finite resources, preoccupation with growth must stop or this, with other factors, could lead to human extinction.

LEARNING ASSESSMENT TEST
(A TEST SIMULATION FOR USE WITH ESS STEP 3)

Part A: Matching

_e_ 1. Preventive checks

_c_ 2. Group migration

_p_ 3. Human ecology

_a_ 4. Fertility

_R_ 5. Immigration

_M_ 6. Momentum

_b_ 7. China

_i_ 8. Population

_f_ 9. Population pyramid

_K_ 10. Crude birth rate

_o_ 11. Pronatalism

_a_ 12. Pull factors

_J_ 13. Kenya

_f_ 14. Emigration

_d_ 15. Mortality

   a. Considerations that draw people to a new geographical location because of the promise of a better life

   b. A country that has achieved significant population control

   c. Occurs when those who share common cultural bonds migrate together to retain group or cultural identity

   d. The number of deaths in a population as measured by mortality rates

   e. The factors of postponed marriage and sexual abstinence as stated by Thomas Malthus

   f. A summary chart of age and sex compositions in a population

   g. The number of births in a population as measured by fertility rates

   h. The biological potential for reproduction

   i. The total number of persons who inhabit a country or territory

   j. A country with severe problems of high fertility and population growth

   k. The total number of births per 1000 people in a population in a year

   l. The process of leaving one country to seek settlement in another

m. Increases in a population long after birth and death rates are stabilized

n. The process of coming to a new country to settle

o. A cultural orientation that strongly encourages childbearing

p. The study of the relationship between human populations and their natural environments

Part B: Multiple Choice

16. The first technological revolution to significantly stimulate world population growth was the
    a. agricultural revolution.
    b. industrial revolution.
    c. urban revolution.
    d. ability to make fire.

17. The world human population now numbers over
    a. 1 billion.
    b. 5 billion.
    c. 3 billion.
    d. 7 billion.

18. The total number of births per 1000 women of childbearing age (15 to 44 years) in a population during a given year refers to
    a. fecundity.
    b. the crude birth rate.
    c. momentum.
    d. the fertility rate.

19. The scientific study of population characteristics and change is
    a. dermatology.
    b. pronatalism.
    c. demography.
    d. human ecology.

20. The number of people in a population under 15 and over 65 divided by the number of people between 15 and 65 years of age refers to
    a. the dependency ratio.
    b. life expectancy.
    c. the growth rate.
    d. the population pyramid.

Part C: True or False

21. T F A mega-city is any city with more than 1 million inhabitants.

22. T F According to Thomas Malthus, such indicators as hunger, disease, war, and "vice" were preventive checks on population growth.

23. T F In several African nations and other less developed countries, death rates are very low compared to birth rates.

24. T F At the beginning of the agricultural revolution, there were about 1 billion people inhabiting this planet.

25. T F Life expectancy refers to the number of years a person of a certain age can be expected to live in his or her society.

Test Answers May Be Found on Page 75.

Percentage Score = (Number of items correct × 4) _____.

Chapter 13

Family: Most Basic of Institutions

DESIRED LEARNING OUTCOMES
(A PREVIEW FOR USE WITH ESS STEP 1)

After successful study of this chapter, the student should be able to

1. define *family* as a concept;

2. briefly discuss changes and trends that have affected the American family institution during the past several decades;

3. briefly explain how the American family operates as an institution in modern society as compared with "family" in simple societies;

4. explain what is meant by *family universals* and discuss at least three examples;

5. discuss each of the following aspects of family structure from a cross-cultural perspective: *marriage, mate selection, rules of descent,* and *rules of residence;*

6. (a) explain the focus or thrust of functionalism as an approach used to study the family and (b) discuss what functionalists regard as key family tasks;

7. (a) explain the focus or thrust of conflict theory as an approach used to study the family and (b) discuss what conflict theorists regard as key family issues;

8. (a) explain the focus or thrust of interactionism as an approach used to study the family and (b) discuss its applications;

9. define and discuss *romantic love* as a concept;

10. discuss each of the following variations of the American family today: the *traditional nuclear family,* the *dual-income family,* the *single-parent family,* and the *step-family;*

11. discuss marital breakdown (divorce) as an issue facing the family today;

12. demonstrate a basic understanding concerning *spouse abuse* as a family problem;

13. demonstrate a basic understanding concerning *child abuse* as a family problem; and

14. discuss each of the following alternatives to the American cultural ideal of family: *remaining single, marriage without children,* and *nonmarital cohabitation.*

Note: For specific information on how to address the instructions in these DLOs (e. g., "define," "discuss," "explain," etc.), consult pages 107–111 of the ESS supplement that follows this Study Guide.

DEVELOPMENT OF THE COMPREHENSIVE OUTLINE
(USING SKILLS CONTAINED IN ESS STEP 2)

To master the DLOs for Chapter 13, it is recommended that you outline the chapter as explained in ESS. The following is an example of what the section "Studying the Family: Different Sociological Approaches" might look like after you develop your own outline of it. Since this is the second major heading in the chapter, it is labeled Roman numeral II.

II. Studying the Family: Different Sociological Approaches

  A. Functionalism
    1. Origins and development: Emerged from nineteenth-century work of Spencer and Durkheim (organic analogy). Was later developed in twentieth century by Parsons, Merton, and others.
    2. Chief proposition (focus): Views society as a system that operates (functions) through its various parts (structures) to maintain social order (equilibrium). Change and conflict are seen as disruptive.
    3. Family—a basic part (structure/ institution) of society.
    4. Main family tasks (functions):
      a. *Reproduction.*
      b. *Regulation of sexual expression.*
      c. *Physical care and protection.*
      d. *Socialization.*
      e. *Social placement* (child learns "place" in terms of obligations in social positions—family, school, community, etc.—and finally makes transition to adulthood).
      f. *Emotional support* (for adult as well as child members).

B. Conflict Theory
  1. Origins and development: Emerged from nineteenth-century work of Marx and Engels; saw history as a series of class struggles.
  2. Chief proposition (as related to the family): Marx saw the family as a society in microcosm. Men were the "haves" (bourgeoisie) and women the "have-nots" (proletariat).
  3. Some contemporary sociologists (Skolnick) have similar views: "Patriarchy . . . must be placed alongside feudalism."
  4. Microlevel applications: Key issues
    a. *The nature of family conflict*—A natural outgrowth of any relationship; no conflict may indicate no intimacy.
    b. *Sources of conflict*—Internal (fatigue, illness, emotional upset) or environmental (finances, in-laws, etc.).
    c. *Conflict management*—Since conflict is inevitable, it must be managed successfully.
      Two Approaches (examples of management strategies):
      (1) **Catharsis therapy**—verbal release of hostility felt toward family members in a controlled therapeutic environment; creates safety-valve effect. Critics argue it only encourages more aggression.
      (2) **Constructive argument**—a process in which family members use a series of steps to focus on the problem rather than on personalities; helps to build win-win rather than win-lose solution.
C. Interactionism
  1. Origins and development: Emerged from early twentieth-century work of Cooley and Mead.
  2. Thrust: Focuses on the meaning people assign to the social world around them; also how people symbolically communicate these perceptions of reality to others.
  3. Family applications: Helps explain interpersonal dynamics between family members from a microlevel perspective.
    a. For children—Parents (significant others) help shape child's self-image and perception of family relations.
    b. For young adults—People develop *role expectations* about how they will act as marriage partners and parents (and how their spouses will act as well) based on childhood experiences with their families and others.
    c. For prospective marriage partners—It is important to communicate openly with future spouse to avoid later **role discrepancy,** a source of martial conflict in which expectations about married life are inconsistent with its realities.
    d. For mature adults in a family—Marriage is a process, not a thing. Children, careers, financial obligations, unseen crises and losses, aging, etc. require constant adjustments in perceptions and priorities.
    e. Interactionism as a therapeutic tool—Family counselors and clinicians may use interactionism as a tool to help people understand, maintain, and improve interpersonal relations with their loved ones.

LEARNING ASSESSMENT TEST
(A TEST SIMULATION FOR USE WITH ESS STEP 3)

Part A: Matching

b   1. A divison of labor

j   2. Polyandry

p   3. Role discrepancy

c   4. Latchkey children

a   5. Family

m   6. Nonmarital cohabitation

o   7. Matrilocal residence

n   8. Family of orientation

a   9. Nuclear family

f   10. Endogamy

l   11. Patrilineal descent

e   12. Stepfamily

k   13. Catharsis therapy

i   14. Exogamy

g   15. Neolocal residence

a. Two or more related persons, usually including a married couple, who share a common household

b. A family universal

c. Children who spend large amounts of time alone without adults present

d. A condition in which expectations about married life are inconsistent with its realities

e. A family in which, when two people marry, stepparent and stepsibling relationships are formed

f. A norm that encourages people to marry within certain culturally defined groups

g. A norm that encourages a married couple to live apart from both families after marriage

h. Two or more persons related by blood, marriage, or adoption who live together and cooperate economically

i. A norm that encourages people to marry outside certain culturally defined groups

j. A form of marriage involving one woman and two or more men

k. The verbal release of hostility felt towards family members in a controlled therapeutic setting

l. Kinship and inheritance traced through the father's bloodline

m. An unmarried man and woman in an intimate relationship who share a common residence

n. The nuclear family of socialization that a child is a part of while growing up

o. A norm that encourages a married couple to live with or near the wife's relatives

p. A source of marital conflict in which expectations about married life are inconsistent with its realities

Part B: Multiple Choice

16. Which of the following life-styles or family patterns has been in decline in recent years (in terms of numbers)?
    a. Nonmarital cohabitation.
    b. The number of children per family.
    c. Single-parent families.
    d. Marriage without children.

17. Kinship and inheritance traced through both bloodlines equally is
    a. neolocal residence.
    b. matrilocal residence.
    c. patrilineal descent.
    d. bilateral descent.

18. Which of the following has emerged as a prevalent and institutionalized basis for marriage only during the last few hundred years?
    a. Romantic love.
    b. Procreation of children.
    c. Cementing family alliances.
    d. Protecting inheritance rights for children.

19. A norm in which the couple upon marriage go to live with or near the husband's relatives is
    a. patriarchal residence.
    b. patrilocal residence.
    c. patriarchal authority.
    d. neolocal residence.

20. The variation of American family with the most complex relationships is the
    a. single-parent family.
    b. traditional nuclear family.
    c. stepfamily.
    d. dual-income family.

Part C: True or False

21. T   F   According to most projections, at least one out of every two American children growing up today will spend some time in a single-parent family.

22. T   F   Third-party day care for preschool children is decreasing as a practice in the United States.

23. T   F   Patriarchal authority is emerging as the dominant family authority pattern in the United States.

24. T   F   Marriage by exchange is a form of mate selection involving a social and economic arrangement between the families of the prospective married couple.

25. T   F   Romantic love refers to the idealization of another person based on attachment, commitment, and intimacy.

Test Answers May Be Found on Page 75.

Percentage Score = (Number of items correct × 4) _____.

TBSK: A Test of Basic Sociological Knowledge

Listed below are thirty statements about American society and social behavior in general that are representative of course content in sociology. Information concerning each of these statements is contained in the text. Read each one carefully and then indicate your assessment of it by circling either **True** or **False** (*Note:* Your instructor may ask you to answer on a machine-graded test form. If that is the case, take a Number 2 pencil and fill in either the "A" or "1" space for True, or the "B" or "2" space for False). If directed to do so by your instructor, also answer items 31 through 37 to provide additional background information.

True   **False**   1. Capital punishment has little or no effect in deterring those who commit murder in the United States.

True   **False**   2. Human beings have a number of instincts that help to guide certain forms of behavior.

True   **False**   3. When viewed objectively, it is clear that American standards of morality, justice, and beauty are superior to those of most other cultures.

True   **False**   4. It is likely that a few children have been successfully reared to maturity by animals such as apes or wolves.

True   **False**   5. Firstborn children tend to be higher achievers than their younger brothers and sisters.

True   **False**   6. From early childhood through their eighteenth birthday, children in the United States spend more time in school than in any other activity except sleep.

True   **False**   7. In American society, the blood bond between family members usually is regarded as more important than the marriage bond.

True   **False**   8. The United States is now making the transition to an agrarian society.

True   **False**   9. Those who "make the first move" in initiating contact with others in group settings tend to be less likely to make friends.

True   False   10. Personalized relations with fellow soldiers at the unit level were much less prevalent among American GIs during the Vietnamese conflict than among American fighting men during World War II.

True   False   11. Deviants such as juvenile gang members and prison inmates rarely form close personalized relationships with others of their kind.

True   False   12. Bureaucracy as a form of social organization has existed for thousands of years.

True   False   13. The concept of brainwashing is a myth that exists mainly in movie plots and in the overactive imaginations of some people.

True   False   14. The behavior of most people is significantly influenced by the environment of the large-scale associations (schools, corporations, and so on) in which they participate.

True   False   15. For most Americans living in poverty, being poor is a temporary condition.

True   False   16. The majority of welfare families include only one or two children.

True   False   17. The most important indicator of social class prestige in the United States is wealth.

True   False   18. The biological concept of race as a ''pure type'' is of little or no use in science.

True   False   19. IQ tests do not measure innate capacity or ''intelligence.''

True   False   20. Like the Nazis' treatment of the Jews during World War II, both the use of concentration camps and attempts at extermination have occurred in America, only on a much smaller scale.

True   False   21. Urban legends—such as the story circulated nationwide in the 1980s that Elvis Presley was still alive—are common in America.

True   False   22. Propaganda methods are rarely used in democratic societies like the United States.

True   False   23. It is clear that alcoholism is a disease caused mainly by biological factors.

True   False   24. Astrology is of little or no scientific value in explaining human behavior.

True   False   25. What is considered deviant or antisocial in the United States (such as immorality or crime) is widely accepted in almost all societies throughout the world.

True   False   26. The United States has the lowest infant mortality rate in the world.

True False	27.	World overpopulation is now one of the most serious social problems facing humankind.
True False	28.	Romantic love is regarded as the primary basis for mate selection in most societies.
True False	29.	The most common form of family violence is spouse abuse.
True False	30.	At least 90 percent of all women in the United States who have ever married give birth to at least one child before their 34th birthday.

Additional Background Information

31. AGE: 19 or less = A (1); 20–24 = B (2); 25–29 = C (3); 30–34 = D (4); 35 or older = E (5).

32. SEX: Female = A (1); Male = B (2).

33. COLLEGE STANDING: Freshman = A (1); Sophomore = B (2); Junior = C (3); Senior = D (4); Other = E (5).

34. MAJOR: Business = A (1); Education = B (2); Liberal Arts/ Humanities = C (3); Physical Sciences = D (4); Other = E (5).

35. DID YOU HAVE SOCIOLOGY AS A COURSE IN HIGH SCHOOL? Yes = A (1); No = B (2).

36. IS THIS YOUR FIRST SEMESTER IN COLLEGE? Yes = A (1); No = B (2).

37. IF YOUR PREVIOUS ANSWER WAS YES, DO NOT CONTINUE. IF YOUR PREVIOUS ANSWER WAS NO, HOW MANY TOTAL COLLEGE CREDIT HOURS HAVE YOU COMPLETED? 1–15 = A (1); 16–30 = B (2); 31–45 = C (3); 46–60 = D (4); More than 60 = E (5).

Scoring: Not Knowledgeable = 18 or below
Barely Knowledgeable = 19–21
Basically Knowledgeable = 22–24
Knowledgeable = 25–27
Very Knowledgeable = 28–30

Answers

LEARNING ASSESSMENT TESTS

The answers to the learning assessment tests are listed below, along with the chapter page numbers where the answers may be found.

Chapter 1

1.	h (4)	8.	c (27)	15.	g (29)	22.	T (11)
2.	f (26)	9.	n (23)	16.	a (12)	23.	T (17)
3.	k (24)	10.	p (28)	17.	d (28)	24.	T (19)
4.	i (8)	11.	d (22)	18.	d (8)	25.	F (13)
5.	j (10)	12.	b (13)	19.	a (18)		
6.	l (20)	13.	a (8)	20.	b (21)		
7.	m (12)	14.	o (21)	21.	F (15)		

Chapter 2

1.	d (36)	8.	g (49)	15.	i (52)	22.	T (50)
2.	h (46)	9.	n (51)	16.	a (48)	23.	T (36)
3.	k (57)	10.	l (58)	17.	c (55)	24.	F (56)
4.	o (48)	11.	e (53)	18.	d (55)	25.	F (60)
5.	m (56)	12.	f (47)	19.	c (37)		
6.	p (44)	13.	a (46)	20.	a (44)		
7.	c (51)	14.	b (37)	21.	F (57)		

Chapter 3

1. e (87)	8. i (77)	15. d (74)	22. F (73)
2. j (79)	9. b (79)	16. d (72)	23. T (68)
3. f (68)	10. g (69)	17. c (78)	24. F (81)
4. p (82)	11. n (76)	18. b (80)	25. F (86)
5. a (68)	12. c (73)	19. b (76)	
6. k (78)	13. l (87)	20. a (77)	
7. m (74)	14. h (84)	21. T (69)	

Chapter 4

1. e (115)	8. o (112)	15. f (112)	22. F (110)
2. d (107)	9. g (115)	16. b (102)	23. T (114)
3. l (100)	10. a (97)	17. d (115)	24. T (97)
4. i (103)	11. h (101)	18. a (105)	25. T (103)
5. k (94)	12. b (102)	19. d (102)	
6. j (102)	13. n (104)	20. c (103)	
7. m (105)	14. c (93)	21. F (114)	

Chapter 5

1. b (112)	8. m (136)	15. d (124)	22. T (139)
2. j (138)	9. o (137)	16. c (136)	23. T (140)
3. f (131)	10. n (139)	17. b (130)	24. F (126)
4. i (137)	11. a (141)	18. c (128)	25. F (136)
5. c (125)	12. g (134)	19. a (133)	
6. k (132)	13. e (127)	20. b (140)	
7. l (134)	14. h (135)	21. F (134)	

Chapter 6

1. n (173)	8. b (166)	15. d (169)	22. T (154)
2. c (171)	9. p (171)	16. c (164)	23. F (157)
3. i (166)	10. f (162)	17. a (169)	24. T (161)
4. h (154)	11. k (167)	18. a (162)	25. F (171)
5. g (156)	12. a (169)	19. d (155)	
6. j (162)	13. m (153)	20. b (169)	
7. e (165)	14. l (161)	21. F (167)	

Chapter 7

1.	c	(191)	8.	b	(200)	15.	e	(197)	22. T (189)
2.	o	(194)	9.	l	(200)	16.	c	(184)	23. T (186)
3.	f	(182)	10.	n	(198)	17.	a	(196)	24. T (201)
4.	d	(187)	11.	j	(183)	18.	d	(186)	25. F (198)
5.	m	(186)	12.	g	(189)	19.	a	(186)	
6.	h	(196)	13.	k	(186)	20.	b	(182)	
7.	a	(198)	14.	i	(189)	21.	F	(182)	

Chapter 8

1.	e	(230)	8.	g	(229)	15.	j	(221)	22. F (210)
2.	h	(208)	9.	l	(229)	16.	a	(224)	23. F (208)
3.	a	(220)	10.	b	(229)	17.	b	(212)	24. T (227)
4.	f	(221)	11.	d	(214)	18.	d	(228)	25. T (213)
5.	i	(224)	12.	p	(218)	19.	d	(214)	
6.	k	(217)	13.	n	(223)	20.	c	(227)	
7.	m	(209)	14.	c	(212)	21.	T	(212)	

Chapter 9

1.	c	(237)	8.	k	(236)	15.	l	(239)	22. T (254)
2.	i	(239)	9.	n	(262)	16.	d	(250)	23. T (242)
3.	e	(250)	10.	j	(256)	17.	a	(255)	24. F (238)
4.	g	(262)	11.	f	(244)	18.	c	(242)	25. T (246)
5.	b	(242)	12.	p	(253)	19.	b	(257)	
6.	o	(256)	13.	d	(244)	20.	b	(261)	
7.	a	(260)	14.	h	(261)	21.	F	(258)	

Chapter 10

1.	d	(276)	8.	c	(292)	15.	i	(290)	22. F (277)
2.	p	(269)	9.	f	(275)	16.	b	(270)	23. F (286)
3.	j	(275)	10.	n	(273)	17.	c	(274)	24. T (290)
4.	g	(268)	11.	h	(277)	18.	d	(292)	25. T (279)
5.	k	(279)	12.	o	(275)	19.	a	(269)	
6.	m	(277)	13.	b	(286)	20.	b	(280)	
7.	l	(269)	14.	e	(273)	21.	T	(280)	

Chapter 11

1. i (300)	8. n (320)	15. e (308)	22. T (303)
2. m (306)	9. b (313)	16. b (309)	23. T (320)
3. g (309)	10. h (305)	17. a (315)	24. T (324)
4. p (311)	11. l (307)	18. c (311)	25. F (312)
5. k (312)	12. f (315)	19. b (315)	
6. o (316)	13. j (322)	20. d (317)	
7. c (300)	14. a (312)	21. F (310)	

Chapter 12

1. e (334)	8. i (331)	15. d (340)	22. F (335)
2. c (342)	9. f (346)	16. a (336)	23. T (333)
3. p (348)	10. k (340)	17. b (330)	24. F (337)
4. g (339)	11. o (347)	18. d (340)	25. T (340)
5. n (341)	12. a (341)	19. c (331)	
6. m (344)	13. j (345)	20. a (344)	
7. b (352)	14. l (341)	21. F (338)	

Chapter 13

1. b (361)	8. n (363)	15. g (367)	22. F (377)
2. j (364)	9. a (363)	16. b (360)	23. F (362)
3. p (373)	10. f (366)	17. d (367)	24. T (366)
4. c (377)	11. l (367)	18. a (374)	25. T (374)
5. h (360)	12. e (379)	19. b (367)	
6. m (384)	13. k (372)	20. c (379)	
7. o (367)	14. i (367)	21. T (378)	

TBSK: A Test of Basic Sociological Knowledge

Listed below are the answers to the TBSK, along with the page numbers in the text where the items are discussed.

1. T (14)	9. F(167)	17. F (224)	25. F (301)
2. F (69)	10. T(158)	18. T (246)	26. F (341)
3. F (76)	11. F(159)	19. T (249)	27. T (330)
4. F (97)	12. T(189)	20. T (253)	28. F (360)
5. T (112)	13. F(183)	21. T (280)	29. T (381)
6. F (113)	14. T(182)	22. F (286)	30. F (383)
7. F (135)	15. T(212)	23. F (314)	
8. F (133)	16. T(213)	24. T (311)	

Part Two

Effective Study Skills (ESS): A System for Academic Excellence (Condensed Version)

Preface

Quality is never an accident; it is always the result of high intention, sincere effort, intelligent direction and skillfull execution; it represents the wise choice of many alternatives.

Willa A. Foster

In the next several pages, you will be shown a concise yet comprehensive system for academic success. This approach to study is called ESS, which stands for "Effective Study Skills." It is a skill-based system designed to furnish you with the "intelligent direction" mentioned above in the quotation by Foster. As such, ESS represents the culmination of almost a decade of research by the author and the experiences of more than 2000 students who served as test subjects. Foster's other three ingredients necessary for quality performance, namely, "high intention," "sincere effort," and "skillful execution," lie within the individual. A person with these characteristics has made the commitment needed for excellence and believes strongly in the old adage that "practice makes perfect."

If you are willing to make such a commitment, then read on. You have the correct attitude for success, and you will find ESS to be indispensable in equipping you with the principles and skills you will need to excel as a student. You may already be an "A" or "B" student who, through intuition or trial and error, has discovered some of the principles and skills contained in ESS. If this is the case, acquisition of the entire ESS system will make you an even better student because, besides learning additional techniques, you will also learn how to order and prioritize your study skills. By comparison, if you lack the commitment to "high intention," "sincere effort," and "skillful execution" or the commitment to develop them, then the "intelligent direction" furnished by ESS will be of little or no value to you.

TEN ACTION PRINCIPLES FOR STUDENT EFFECTIVENESS

As a prerequisite for the successful use of ESS, you will need to accept and implement the following action principles until they become internalized as values about college life and manifested as everyday student behavior:

1. **Use a Collegiate Dictionary** — Increasing your vocabulary is an essential component of your college education. Every student should use a college-level dictionary, which is available at any college bookstore. When an instructor or author uses an unfamiliar word, you can then look it up to increase your word skills and broaden your understanding.

2. **Develop the Habit of Never Missing Class** — Almost without exception, students who consistently make A's rarely if ever miss a class. They know from experience that daily attendance is essential to derive the maximum benefit from a class. In contrast, the student who misses classes should not expect to earn above average grades, and the student who misses excessively should not expect to complete the term with a passing grade.

3. **Take Responsibility for Your Academic Performance** — College students are expected to assume the responsibilities that accompany the college experience. Most college instructors have neither the time nor the inclination to supervise students closely concerning the completion of every assignment. Likewise, it is the exceptional instructor who checks on the daily progress of students and their study habits. Therefore, the student is usually left to his or her own resources and is expected to take full responsibility and schedule study time carefully to meet all requirements and earn acceptable grades.

4. **Engage in Constructive Class Participation** — Successful students find it advantageous to work with their instructors to create a positive learning environment. College professors, being human, respond best and usually teach a better class when students meet them halfway by cooperating and participating in class. Techniques you can use to enhance this process and gain the maximum benefit from your instructors and their classes include the following:

   a. *Always arrive at class on time.*

   b. *Sit in the front row* or near the front of the classroom in order to see and hear everything more clearly. This will (1) keep you more alert and thus less likely to daydream or go to sleep and (2) decrease the likelihood of your being distracted by the fidgeting or whispering of nonserious students, which tends to be more pronounced toward the back rows. Since relatively few students strive for excellence and an A grade, you can usually find a front-row seat. If your instructor uses a seating chart, request to sit in the front row or near the front.

   c. *Have your notebook open and be prepared to take notes when each class begins.*

   d. *Avoid conduct that is distracting to other students,* such as irrelevant conversation, whispering, eating, drinking, chewing gum, and so forth.

   e. *Participate constructively in class discussions and ask questions* of your instructor, particularly if you do not understand a key concept or point and need further clarification.

5. **Complete Required Reading before Class** — Instructors assume that their students have read all appropriate assignments prior to the class session in which such material may be discussed. Yet at least one-half of all first-year college students lag behind and do not stay current with their reading assignments. *Successful students complete their reading assignments ahead of time* and, therefore, have their learning reinforced when much of the same material is then covered in class lecture or discussion. In this manner, they derive the maximum benefit from each class.

6. **Take Comprehensive Class Notes** — Students who perform well take extensive notes in class. This is an essential habit to develop, because many instructors include additional material in their class presentations that is not in the text or other required reading. Students who take detailed notes benefit because the class reinforces what they learn from their reading, and they also receive helpful clues regarding information that is likely to appear on an exam.

   How to take notes effectively. Many if not most college instructors talk at a fairly brisk, conversational pace. Therefore, *do not try to write down every word that is said.* This will not only frustrate you, it will also result in the accumulation of a great deal of nonessential information that will have to be sifted and sorted through later. Successful students use techniques for note taking that allow them to capture the essence of the material covered in class. Some of the most helpful of these techniques are listed below:

   a. *Listen carefully to what is being said and how it is being presented.* Use these guidelines and techniques for maximum success:

      (1) *Focus your attention on identifying core or essential material* such as key concepts, principles and theories, and important thinkers and personalities.

      (2) *Recognize that things repeated by the instructor—mentioned more than once— are done so for emphasis.* You are likely to see these areas of content again on an exam.

      (3) *Consider anything written on the blackboard to be likely material for exam questions.*

      (4) *Mentally summarize explanations of core material in a concise form.* If, for example, your instructor spends five minutes explaining and illustrating a concept or principle, listen rather than try to write down every word. Then, mentally summarize it in only a few words, phrases, or sentences, and write this down.

   b. *Write class notes in a concise, organized manner.* Follow these tips for maximum success.

      (1) *Develop your own form of shorthand.* Practice leaving out nonessential words such as adverbs, adjectives, and prepositions. It is also helpful to develop a system of abbreviations and acronyms that have meaning for you. For example, an American history instructor will use terms such as "American," "political," and "Monroe Doctrine" dozens of times if not more. Abbreviations such as "Am,"

"pol," and "MoDoc" will serve just as well for note-taking purposes. Likewise, you could use the even more efficient acronym "MD" for Monroe Doctrine.

(2) *Write class notes in the form of an outline.* Although it will take some time and effort to master the skill of outlining, the rewards will be well worth the effort. The class material will be in a concise, coherent form that you will be able to master much more easily for exams.

(3) *Abandon the use of a tape recorder* as soon as possible (if you use one). It is not advisable for most students to tape-record class lectures even though some instructors allow it. Although the beginning student may find tape-recorded lectures to be self-assuring because "I got it all," such "security blankets" are in reality inefficient and ineffective ways to learn in most circumstances. For most learners, recording is a poor substitute for good note-taking skills that allow the student to "get it right" the first time when the class is held.

7. **Practice Effective Time Management** — College study is a serious enterprise that requires an adequate amount of time to achieve academic success. Experts agree that *most successful students look upon a full course load of 12 to 16 semester hours as a full-time job responsibility that requires a similar amount of commitment and work.* Therefore, you will need to spend approximately **two hours of study outside class for every hour spent in class** in order to succeed and excel in college. Some students are able to barely get by and earn passing grades with a commitment of smaller amounts of time. However, if you wish to excel in school and get A grades, you will need to put in at least this amount of time.

8. **Follow Instructions** — To achieve maximum success, it is important for the student to follow carefully the instructions established for each course. *It is common in higher education for first- and second-year college students to lose points or even letter grades simply because they do not follow instructions.* Therefore, use the following guidelines to maximize the points you will receive and thus earn the best grade possible:

   a. *Always attend the first day of class.* Many students register late or fail to attend the first day of class because they mistakenly figure "nothing will be covered." In truth, *the first day is the most important day, with the possible exception of the day of the final exam.* This is when the requirements and tone are established for the rest of the term. Some professors give instructions orally and do not give a course syllabus. They expect students to take notes on the course requirements. Others give only a very general one-page syllabus and fill in the details verbally. Just as important, students who miss the first class or two usually fail to get the reading assignment and often have to play "catch up" until at least the first exam is given.

   b. *Read the course syllabus carefully and refer to it as necessary during the semester.* It is your responsibility to ask for a syllabus if you register late or otherwise miss the first day. This becomes the blueprint of the course to follow.

   c. *Read exam instructions carefully.* Particularly in essay exams, pay close attention to what the question asks for.

    d. Follow instructions for papers and projects to the letter. Many instructors have their own formats for writing research papers, book reviews, and other assignments. Make sure you understand what is being called for and that your work is organized exactly as specified. Often, otherwise excellent papers are marked down simply because the student did not follow instructions. There is no hope of obtaining an A grade, or sometimes even a B or C, from most professors unless you do this.

    e. Never miss a deadline. Part of the self-discipline required for maximum success in college involves learning to pace yourself and properly manage your time. *Begin papers and projects early in the term and complete them early if at all possible.* You will need the last few days before the end of the semester to prepare for final exams. Many professors deduct substantially for work turned in late, and some will grant no credit at all. Students should understand that teachers are busy at the end of the semester too. They have to set deadlines so that they can evaluate all work and meet deadlines imposed on them for turning in grades.

9. **Prepare Required Papers and Projects as If You Were Applying for a Job** — Those who become successful in obtaining full-time positions realize that appearances count in applying for and interviewing for jobs. In the competitive world we live in, few employers hire people who turn in incomplete and sloppy applications and resumes or dress and act inappropriately at interviews. A successful applicant takes the extra steps to convince the prospective employer that he or she is the best person for the job. From the employer's vantage point, those who exhibit such characteristics are also more likely to take pride in their work and do an excellent job.

    College students also live in a competitive world in terms of grades. To get the best grade on a research paper, book review, or other written project, appearances do matter. Those who earn A's almost always take extra pains to make sure all written work is neatly typed with correct spelling, grammar, and punctuation.

    Professors may read hundreds of papers each semester. They assume, and rightly so, that the best ones almost always stand out from the crowd in appearance and form as well as in content. *Students who take pride in how their work looks usually take the same care in making sure the content of their work is superior.* **Excellence is an attitude and a habit.** Those who practice it adopt it as a way of life and are constantly trying to do their best and improve upon their "best" in all areas. This attitude is reflected in the quality of work people do. Employers recognize this quality in job applicants who are hired, and professors look for it in the few students who earn A's. *If you will implement this principle, it will help you to earn A's too.*

10. **"Study Smart" for Final Exams** — At the college level, the entire semester's work in a course tends to build toward the final exam, which is the culmination of several months of effort. Many instructors give comprehensive finals that cover the entire semester from the first day on. Final exam scores constitute a major part of your grade and, in many instances, count more than anything else. Therefore, focus your study efforts toward preparation for the final exam, particularly if it is comprehensive. As you progress through the semester or term, keep your study notes for each course organized and store them all in the same place for easy retrieval later. Most important, *start your*

study for final exams well ahead of time. Final exam week can be hectic. Many students who end up with mediocre or failing grades do so because they become overwhelmed as a result of their own procrastination and lack of organization. You can avoid this by "studying smart" and organizing your time and materials carefully.

THE FOUR STEPS OF ESS: AN INTRODUCTION

To achieve maximum success, a student must acquire a specific set of study skills, to be developed and implemeted in a particular sequence as a total learning system. This is where ESS comes in. ESS, which stands for "Effective Study Skills," identifies the essential skills needed to achieve peak performance as a learner in an academic setting and demonstrates how to use them in a simple four-step process. If you are willing to work hard and devote a semester or two toward the complete mastery of these skills, you will experience significant, if not dramatic, improvement in your ability to grasp and master course material. Your grade-point average will rise accordingly.

As I pursued graduate studies in sociology with a special interest in the sociology of education, I studied the literature in both the sociology and psychology of learning. It became clear that a concise, skill-based study system for college students that really worked was greatly needed. There have been, of course, such approaches as "the SQ3R method" by Francis Robinson (1946) and the more recent book by Gordon Green (1985), *Getting Straight A's.* While these approaches and others like them do identify some of the skills needed for academic success, they are, regrettably, largely conceptual in nature and tend to lack the comprehensive and systematic nature of a truly effective study system that focuses on the building of skills in a coherent step-by-step manner.

To meet the need for such a concise yet comprehensive study system, ESS was developed. ESS is designed to (1) meet the needs of students for a clear, concise system with which to learn and master all essential skills needed for academic success in most areas of college study, (2) provide students with a step-by-step procedure for using the skills, and (3) show students how to evaluate their level of skill usage so that, ultimately, mastery of all skill elements can be achieved and A grades can be obtained. *To achieve significant benefit from ESS, the student should have reading, writing, and math skills at the appropriate level to take academic college level courses.* Assuming this, diligent application of the entire ESS system should result in mastery of all essential skills and superior academic performance.

It should be stressed that ESS is not designed to show marginal students a series of shortcuts to enable them to "survive" in college. This is the approach used by some so-called study systems advertised on television. Instead, *ESS teaches students how to achieve academic excellence.* To achieve success at college is a serious responsibility that requires a great deal of commitment and hard work. There are no shortcuts or easy ways to achieve academic excellence. The superior student will spend a minimum of two hours of study each week outside class for every hour spent in class. The purpose of ESS is to show the student how to make the most effective and efficient use of that study time for maximum learning and peak performance on exams. If this is done, there are no limits to how far the skills learned in ESS can take the practitioner. Some ESS users have not only earned four-year degrees, but have gone on successfully to pursue studies in graduate and professional schools as well.

It normally takes typical students six months to one year to fully master all the skills taught in ESS. After one year, many of those who diligently implement this system perform on a level that qualifies them for the dean's list. However, most ESS users experience significant if not dramatic improvements in their study skills within a few short weeks. In other words, improved grade performance occurs almost immediatey in most cases. But more important, course content is more readily retained in long-term memory, and ESS practitioners are on their way to becoming much more effective learners and better-educated people.

In the pages that follow, ESS is fully explained. I used this system myself to complete a doctorate at North Texas State University (now University of North Texas) with a 4.0 grade-point average. You can do the same in your undergraduate studies and make straight A's just as I did. All it requires is work and some patience on your part as you develop the skills. I like to think of ESS as a key that can open the door to academic success. It certainly has benefited me and thousands of students across the country. It can do the same for you.

ESS is a generic system that is effective in most academic and professional college courses. These include courses in anatomy and physiology, anthropology, business and accounting, biology, botany, economics, geology, geography, history, nursing, philosophy, political science, psychology, sociology, and zoology. With some slight fine-tuning by the student, ESS can also work for courses such as chemistry, English, physics, and mathematics.

The four steps in the ESS system are as follows:

ESS: A System for Academic Excellence

Step 1: Textbook Usage Skills

Step 2: Content Organization Skills

Step 3: Exam Preparation Skills

Step 4: Diagnostic Follow-up

As you read on, keep in mind that ESS is a total, skill-based system that must be implemented in the following manner for maximum success: *Use the first three steps contained in ESS every time you prepare for a major exam in each of your courses. If, for example, you take a political science or biology course that includes three major exams and a comprehensive final, you will need to use the system four times in that course.* The use of Step 4, Diagnostic Follow-up, is usually needed only during the first semester or two as the student develops mastery of the skills. After ESS is fully mastered, Step 4 will cease to be necessary in most cases.

ESS is extremely meaty with very little filler. Therefore, it is to be studied carefully and savored like a fine meal at a four-star restaurant rather than "wolfed down" on the run like a hamburger at a "fast food joint." If the sheer richness of the ESS diet of principles, steps, skills, and tasks starts to overwhelm you, slow down and deal with the material a section at a time. If you will begin to implement the skill of *active reading* (Step 1 of ESS) as you read through the next several pages, you should have no problem.

STEP 1: TEXTBOOK USAGE SKILLS

Have you ever found yourself reading an important assignment but being unable to stay awake even though you had had plenty of sleep the night before? Did you just keep nodding off every fifteen or twenty minutes? Have you ever been reading a text assignment only to find that after twenty or thirty minutes, your mind had begun to wander? Finally, have you ever tried diligently to read a lengthy textbook chapter and, after what seemed like an eternity, started thumbing over to the end to count the pages left before you could finish the darn thing?

If any of this sounds familiar, then you have exhibited one or more symptoms of the passive reading syndrome, a problem that afflicts many students. This problem often plagues those who must read academic and technical literature and is particularly common among first- and second-year college students. It happens to many students who, in making the abrupt change from high school to college, are sometimes unfamiliar with the special qualities and challenges of college-level material.

Simply defined, **the passive reading syndrome** *is unfocused academic or technical reading with low comprehension and retention.* It occurs when the reader (1) lacks a clearly identified goal concerning the material at hand and (2) does not possess or put to use the skills and procedures necessary to attain it. For college students who fall into this trap, passive reading involves going through the motions of completing the reading assignment with very little learning taking place. Have you, for example, ever read a textbook chapter and then said to yourself, "I read it, but I don't remember much of anything about it"?

If this has happened to you, you may have done what many students try to do to remedy the situation. You just read it again. Consequently, many first- and second-year students tend to experience some frustration with textbooks because the material seems to wash over their brains like waves on a beach. It does not "sink in" or have much impact in terms of learning. In some cases, a student may read a chapter over for a second or even third time without significant success. The first step in ESS—Textbook Usage Skills—is designed to address this and several other reading concerns.

Textbook Usage Skills are the ones acquired first in the ESS system. This is because, in most cases, the first important task your instructor gives you when you enter class the first day is a textbook or other reading assignment. This and other such assignments that follow are important because, *in first- and second-year survey courses, the textbook usually furnishes the foundation for the course and often represents the primary source of course content that the student will be tested on later.*

To master the effective use of textbooks and other required reading material, you must acquire four basic skills which are to be used each time in their proper order, and a fifth, time management, which ties them together. This sequential use of all steps and skills contained in the system is necessary because ESS is designed to increase and reinforce learning continuously as you prepare for each exam. The five basic skills of successful textbook usage are as follows:

Step 1: Textbook Usage Skills

a. Active Reading

    b. **Identifiation of Core Material**

    c. **Topical Mapping**

    d. **Chapter Outlining**

    e. **Time Management**

a. Active Reading

As a college or university student, you must approach text assignments in a different manner than you would any other form of reading. Compared with novels and other casual forms of recreational reading, textbooks lack the suspense and plot development that so often capture the attention of fiction readers. Some college texts are rather dry and matter-of-fact in their form of presentation. This is because their authors have developed them with a very different set of objectives in mind. Of the greatest importance for you is the fact that you will be tested on the textbook material and evaluated as a student on the basis of the grades you earn. Therefore, it is essential that you acquire the skill of active reading as an effective means of dealing with these materials for maximum academic success.

    For the purposes of ESS, **active reading** *is defined as focused reading with (1) a clearly identified goal and (2) a set of effective steps or procedures that are used to attain it.* As a student, your goal in dealing with textbooks and all other reading assignments is to identify, categorize, and fully understand the different types of content material for which you will be held responsible on exams. In this regard, active reading is the first and most important textbook usage skill you will develop. Your success in acquiring and using the other four skills of core material identification, topical mapping, chapter outlining, and time management will depend upon your active reading ability.

    Active reading is task-oriented in nature, with a set of step-by-step procedures you will need to follow in order to identify and master the material you will be tested on. It is perhaps best to handle reading assignments on a chapter-by-chapter basis, because these are the types of reading increments most often assigned by undergraduate instructors. Therefore, the textbook chapter should be actively read using the procedural steps identified below:

    a. **Active Reading (by chapter)**
       Tasks to Perform:

       (1) **Reading Preview**

       (2) **"Chunking" by Chapter Section**

       (3) **Paragraph Classification**

          (a) **Core Material Paragraphs**
             Concepts
             Principles and Theories
             Important Men and Women
             Additional Forms

          (b) **Elaboration Paragraphs**

(1) Reading Preview.   Your first task as an active reader is to preview the material you plan to read. The **reading preview** *is a brief examination of the chapter outline, in the table of contents or in the chapter itself, to orient the reader to the material that will be read.* This helps to give the student direction and focus in seeing the "big picture" presented by the assignment. Thus, the reading preview furnishes the student with clues as to how the central idea or theme presented by the chapter will be explained.

Unfortunately, many beginning students approach their college assignments like other nonacademic forms of reading. They simply plunge forth into the chapter by reading it with no focus or direction. Then, after completing it, they find that they do not know where they have been, why they have been there, and what they were supposed to have learned. In many cases, this is not their fault, but occurs because no one has taught them that academic material is different from other forms of reading and must be approached differently. Therefore, they unwittingly fall into the passive reading trap and can become very frustrated by reading text assignments over and over again with little apparent success.

You can conduct a reading preview in a couple of basic ways. First of all, most authors of first- and second-year college texts include a brief outline of each chapter either in the table of contents (at the beginning of the book) or at the beginining of each chapter. These outlines are placed there intentionally to furnish you, the student, with a set of guideposts to follow in acquainting yourself with the chapter's key idea, theme, or topic and the material contained within, as organized in the form of headings and subheadings. Second, if there is no such chapter outline in the table of contents, you can take a few minutes to thumb through the chapter and examine the sections and subsections and topics and subtopics. Most first- and second-year texts are designed to assist you in this respect by separating the major sections and subsections of the chapter from the body of the text in the form of headings and subheadings. They are typically printed in raised print and boldface type (larger, italicized, or darker letters).

Therefore, before reading any textbook assignment, take a few minutes to study the outline to become oriented to the reading that follows. If you find it helpful, write down a few ideas to summarize what you think the chapter is about in terms of the "what, where, when, who, why, and how" questions that might apply. This will provide focus to your reading. In addition, the questions that you formulate here represent the important ideas in the chapter that you may see again on an exam.

(2) "Chunking" by Chapter Section.   Once your reading preview is completed, you then proceed to **"chunking" by chapter section,** the next active reading task. This is *a process in which a larger amount of content material (for instance, a textbook chapter) is divided into smaller increments or sections for more effective learning.* Researchers who study how learning occurs have found that the most effective and efficient learning usually takes place in small increments or "little wholes." Some learning theorists refer to this process as "chunking," the dividing of larger learning tasks into smaller ones. When you engage in an activity as complex as academic or technical reading, it is important to have a plan of attack, a blueprint, or a strategy to follow. Just as the successful mountain climber does not merely grab some equipment and start climbing, the successful college student should not just pick up a textbook and start reading without a detailed plan in mind in terms of how to proceed.

The authors of first- and second-year college texts divide each chapter into three or four, five or six, and sometimes seven or eight major sections or "chunks." This division of the chapter into smaller learning components is designed for your benefit to assist you in clearly understanding the topic presented in the chapter. Consequently, you need to focus your reading on these sections or "chunks" as you build, step by step, toward completion and understanding of the entire chapter.

(3) Paragraph Classification. As you focus your attention first on one section or "chunk" of the chapter and then another, you will next need to learn and implement **paragraph classification,** the most important task in active reading. *This involves the analysis of reading content at the paragraph level to distinguish core material from elaboration.* You might think of this as "chunking" at the paragraph level. So, you begin to read a chapter and concentrate your efforts initially on the first section or "chunk" (as represented by the first major heading). Simultaneously, you focus your attention on each paragraph contained in the section to determine whether it contains basically core material, elaboration, or, in some cases, both.

Core material *is the essential course content that forms the basis for exam questions.* In college courses, core material may come from several sources: the textbook, the instructor's lectures, and additional sources such as collateral readers, material placed on library reserve, and so forth. This will be discussed at length in Step 2 of ESS which follows. However, in the context of active reading discussed here, *core material* refers to all essential course content in a textbook.

A **core material paragraph** *is any paragraph in a college reading assignment that introduces a key portion of content which could appear again on an exam.* Such paragraphs may also contain some elaboration designed to explain the meaning of an essential concept or other form of core material to the reader. However, core material paragraphs should be distinguished from elaboration paragraphs, which serve a different purpose, namely to illuminate and expand upon essential material.

Such core material forms the foundation for both the course and the exams upon which the final course grade will be determined. Since core material paragraphs are typically (1) fewer than those designed to clarify and elaborate and (2) most important for study and test purposes, the ability to distinguish the difference between them and elaboration paragraphs is essential to mastering the skill of active reading.

Also important to the student is the ability to recognize and understand the **different types of core material.** These include concepts, principles and theories, important men and women and their contributions, and additional forms that relate to the specific nature of some subjects and courses. **Concepts** *are key terms an author uses for important ideas, which usually involve very precise definitions.* As such, they represent agreements among scholars concerning the meaning of the phenomena they investigate. The ancient Greeks were among the first to conceptualize ideas precisely. They, for example, agreed on three concepts of love: *philos* (long-lasting, deep friendship), *eros* (sexual attraction), and *agape* (nondemanding spiritual love). **Principles and theories** *consist of the structuring of meaningful relationships among concepts and facts at different levels of complexity and scope.* Examples might include "Bowden's reflex principle of real-world markets" in economics, or "binary fission theory" in biology. **Important men and women** *are listed and discussed in* *college course material in terms of their contributions to history, the humanities, and science.* Core material may also take several **additional forms,** depending on the subject or course involved. For example, a particular formula or group of formulas or equations would represent special forms of core material in algebra or calculus. Likewise, various systems (such as skeletal, digestive, and respiratory) and their elements along with phyla and their categories and subcategories would represent special forms of core material in biology.

Elaboration material *consists of examples, illustrations, explanations, and additional forms of detail that act to clarify and expand upon the core information presented in a text or other college reading material.* Although elaboration material may not be the focus on many, if not most, college exams, it is nonetheless very important. If the student, for example, is adept at identifying and memorizing definitions or lists of core material without understanding (1) what the core material means and (2) the relationships between and among different concepts, principles, and theories, then he or she may do poorly on exams. *College level work is higher education. This means that students will, in many cases, be expected to demonstrate the analytical skills of critical thinking.* They will be expected at times to analyze, synthesize, compare, and contrast different forms of core material on exams as well as apply what they have learned to a novel situation to further test their analytical skills.

An **elaboration paragraph** *is any paragraph that explains, illustrates, clarifies, and otherwise expands upon core material.* Because such paragraphs act to illuminate and "flesh out" the skeleton presented by core material, they tend to be more numerous. Consequently, they comprise the bulk of most first- and second-year college texts. As a guideline or "rule of thumb" to follow, there tends to be at least one or two (sometimes three or four) elaboration paragraphs for every core material paragraph, depending on the particular course and the author's style of writing. This is important to know, as all core material needs to be dealt with very differently from elaboration material for effective textbook usage.

b. Identification of Core Material

This textbook usage skill employs and builds directly on the skill of active reading. The overlap, in terms of the use of skills in subsequent components and steps in ESS, is designed to build study skill acquisition to a mastery level as soon as possible. Thus skills are first introduced and then applied in a cumulative fashion, so that there is constant reinforcement as the student progresses through the various skills and steps of the system. In this manner, not only is the skill of active reading, for example, used to effectively master other sources of course reading such as library assignments on reserve, but elements of it can also be used to implement more easily the active listening skills needed to master the taking of comprehensive class notes (see Action Principle for Student Effectiveness Number 6).

Identification of core material *is a process whereby all essential information from the reading assignment that could appear on the exam is clearly identified.* This is an extremely important skill to master because, with this ability, the student can reduce the most voluminous reading assignments to a concise form for effective exam preparation. Core material from reading assignments that will appear on exams can be identified through the completion of the following steps:

b. **Identification of Core Material (to appear on exam)**
    Tasks to Perform:

    (1) **Active Reading**

    (2) **Use of Learning Aids in Text**

        (a) **Headings and Subheadings**

        (b) **Boldface and Italicized Words**

        (c) **Chapter Summaries**

        (d) **Glossaries of Important Terms**

        (e) **Review Questions**

    (3) **Use of Student Study Guide (optional)**

(1) Active Reading. First, you must fully implement the skill of active reading that has already been discussed. In short, this involves the tasks of reading preview, "chunking" by chapter section, and paragraph classification. This allows you to divide the reading material into smaller and smaller units for easier learning. At the most elementary level of paragraph classification, you must separate core material paragraphs from elaboration paragraphs and, by doing so, identify key concepts, principles and theories, important men and women, and perhaps other forms of core material that are likely to appear on an exam. If you do this correctly, not only will you be able to dissect a reading assignment, but you will also see how the various elements of core material at the paragraph level combine and build to make up the key "chunks" or chapter sections for a clear understanding of the chapter as a whole. In essence, this is how you use action reading skills.

(2) Use of Learning Aids in Text. To facilitate the identification of core material likely to appear on exams, you should make use of the **learning aids** that appear in most first- and second-year college texts. Authors place these aids in texts to assist students in identifying much of the essential material that they will be tested on later.

　　Such aids include headings and subheadings, boldface and italicized words, chapter summaries, glossaries of important terms, and review questions. *Chapter headings and subheadings* essentially do the "chunking" for you, in that they divide the chapter material into key sections and subsections. In this regard, they are the basic building blocks of each chapter. In many instances, such headings and subheadings point the way by providing you with clues as to the forms of core material to look for. *Boldface and italicized words* cause the various forms of core material, such as key concepts or principles, to stand out from the rest of the text. Each is usually followed by a brief definition, essential to understanding what the emphasized word means. A *chapter summary,* when used, appears at the end of the chapter and states in condensed form the essential content of the chapter. A *glossary of important terms,* likewise, may appear at the end of a chapter and serves to identify and briefly define for the student many of the important concepts found in the chapter. As an additional study aid, authors of some survey texts include *review questions* at the end of chapters to test the student's acquisition of core material.

(3) Use of Student Study Guide. As an optional step, you may wish to make use of the **student study guide** that is available with some first- and second-year texts. The primary purpose of such a guide is to assist the student in the identification and acquisition of core material. In many instances, it is a small book designed to go along with your text, available at extra cost at your college bookstore. A few texts, however, contain their own study guides that are placed at the back of a book as a supplement. The use of a study guide may be helpful to a beginning student. *It often contains such learning aids as detailed learning objectives on which to focus study, chapter outlines, and learning assessment tests with sample questions similar to those that could appear on a real exam.*

Learning aids designed into texts and study guides are very useful to first- and second-year college students. Use them and benefit from them. However, heed the following words of caution. *Learning aids ideally should be used just as the name implies, as aids to check your own ability to distinguish core material on your own.* Unfortunately, some students, particularly those with negative first experiences with college texts, fall into the habit of using such devices as "crutches" in an attempt to take shortcuts. Therefore, they often do not read their text assignments thoroughly. Not only do such students tend to perform at a mediocre level during their first two years at college, but they experience a rude awakening if and when they become juniors.

During the junior and senior years at college, most learning aids disappear from required text material. At this level, the student is expected to have good study habits and to be able to perform as an independent learner. Professors may also tend to place increasing emphasis on original sources. For example, in a freshman survey course in psychology, you are typically told about the basic contributions of such theorists as Watson, Freud, and Skinner. At the junior and senior levels, however, your psychology professor may assign long excerpts or books written by selected theorists in the field.

While it is true that at the junior and senior levels, much if not most coursework will be in your major and minor fields (in which you have the greatest interest), you nevertheless will be exposed to much reading material written by scholars for other scholars. Such material usually is devoid of the learning aids that characterize first- and second-year survey texts. So, if you have plans to complete a four-year degree or perhaps even pursue graduate studies, *be advised that it will be you versus the print on the page.* Consequently, now is the time to develop your study skills to a mastery level. If you do, there will be no limit to what you will be able to accomplish in your future studies.

c. Topical Mapping

Once you have begun successfully to separate core material from elaboration material and to identify the key concepts, principles and theories, important men and women, and other essential material, it is time to separate, clearly and visibly, core material from elaboration. In other words, you will be tested on the essence or "meat" of the material in your text. So it is now time to separate the meat from the "fat" for the purposes of maximum learning and effective exam preparation. To accomplish this with the greatest success, you must master the skill of topical mapping.

Topical mapping *refers to (1) the visible separation of core material from elaboration* *material in the text so that both can easily be identified and (2) the reduction of such material to the most concise form possible for effective learning.* This is an active, task-oriented way to approach the material contained in a textbook so that maximum learning can take place. Topical mapping thus points the way through or "maps" the chapter for future study. It involves the following procedures that are summarized here:

    c. Topical Mapping
        Tasks to Perform:

        (1) **Strategic Highlighting (core material)**

        (2) **Analytical Summary (elaboration material)**

(1) Strategic Highlighting. **Strategic highlighting** *is using a colored pen or marker to highlight or underline core material precisely.* To avoid confusion and keep things simple, it is advisable in most cases to use a highlighter pen of only one color. Students today often use colored pens or markers to highlight what they consider important text material. However, many of them highlight far too much material. In this regard, the author occasionally has observed beginning students who appear to take their text in one hand and their highlighter pen in the other and, like the swashbuckling swordsman Zorro in the movies, make bold strokes with the pen, not unlike those made with a sword. When fully one-fourth to one-half of each page is highlighted in this manner, the student has defeated his or her own purpose.

    Instead, you must learn to highlight such material with precision. *If you highlight more than 15 percent of the total text, you are highlighting too much; 10 percent should be more than sufficient in most cases.* Just as the Olympic target shooter uses a rifle to hit the bull's-eye every time, you too can use your highlighter pen in similar fashion to make a perfect score in regard to core material, instead of wielding it like a shotgun to splatter the page with vivid color. Specifically then, *all you should highlight is the precise term or phrase that represents, for example, a key concept or principle and perhaps the one- or two-line definition or capsule explanation that usually accompanies it.* If the core material takes the form of a complex theory or event, then it may be necessary to highlight the essential causes, elements, or propositions that follow. However, in most cases, anything else will most likely be elaboration material that should be handled in a different way.

(2) Analytical Summary. At least 85 to 90 percent of all material contained in first- and second-year textbooks is elaboration material that is important in its own right. Without a firm grasp of the elaboration in the form of examples and illustrations, anecdotes, in-depth explanations, and so on, the core material would have little or no meaning or significance. An effective and efficient way to organize such material is through **analytical summary,** *a process in which the student makes brief marginal notes that summarize elaboration material.* As you move through your reading assignment and engage in the highlighting of core material, take time to read carefully the elaboration material that follows. Read it in terms of how it supports and explains the concept or other core material you have just highlighted. Then *take a moment to reflect on it and, in just a word, a phrase, or at most a sen-*

marize it and write your own brief analysis in the margin of your book on the same page. If you find it useful, use a special pen to record such notes to yourself. If you find it necessary to keep track of which notes go with which highlighted material, draw a small arrow from your marginal comments to the highlighted material it explains.

This entire process of topical mapping (strategic highlighting and analytical summary) will be of tremendous value to you in understanding and retaining the material in your textbook. *The primary benefit of highlighting core material is that you are able to pinpoint precisely the essential text material that exam questions come from.* Also, because of the active, task-oriented manner in which you use this skill, your mind will much more readily grasp and retain the material. This increased learning benefit is also apparent with your use of analytical summary. *By taking only a moment or two to pause, think about what you have read, and then summarize perhaps two or three paragraphs into a phrase or sentence or two as a marginal note, you are engaging in analysis and synthesis. This is task-oriented concentration at a high mental level that promotes effective learning.*

d. Chapter Outlining

The fourth textbook usage skill to be implemented in Step 1 of ESS is chapter outlining. So far, you have seen how the effective use of text material begins with active reading. This, in turn, leads to the identification of core material and topical mapping. The next skill, **chapter outlining** *is a process in which all essential reading content is brought together into a logical framework within the text to provide the mind of the student with the logical structure it needs for more effective learning.* It is briefly outlined as follows:

> d. Chapter Outlining
>   Tasks to Perform:
>
>   (1) Use Outline Notation
>
>   (2) Use Color Coding

(1) Use Outline Notation. To simplify chapter outlining as much as possible, *complete the outline in the book.* To begin, use **outline notation** by *adding Roman numerals, capital letters, and so forth to the material already in the text to give it more structure and coherent organization.* Suppose you are taking a course in the first half of American history. Your reading assignment for this week is a chapter on the Civil War period. So far, you have implemented the textbook usage skills of active reading, identification of core material, and topical mapping and wish to complete the process by outlining the chapter in the book. To do so, go to the first "chunk" or section of the chapter and start your outline there. Then look at the first major heading in that section. Often such headings give clues about the core material to follow and how to organize it. In this case, if the major heading says, "The Major Causes of the Civil War," you would make this *Roman numeral I.*

As you proceed through the next few pages devoted to this section, you come across the key elements of core material contained within. Suppose the first cause you have highlighted is "The Dred Scott Decision." This becomes *capital A.* You proceed on through this first chunk, or section, of the chapter, adding capital letters, numerical ones, twos, and threes, and so on until the entire section is outlined. Repeat this process for the entire chapter.

(2) Use Color Coding. For the sake of efficiency and easy identification, use **color coding**. This is using a colored pen to apply outline notation in order to make the chapter outline in the text stand out from the rest of the material. For example, you might use a red pen or pencil and write the Roman numerals, capital letters, numbers, lowercase letters, and so forth either right in with the text or in the margin to the left of the core material you have highlighted.

It should be noted that while chapter outlining may seem to be an unnecessary step to some students since another more comprehensive outline will be constructed later, it should be used for several reasons. First, *chapter outlining should take less than a minute per page once it is fully mastered,* although it will take longer the first few times it is used. The fact that it takes some time in the beginning should tell students that they need to learn how to better organize material into a coherent framework. Second, the ability to arrange content material into a coherent outline requires concentration and the complicated thought processes of analysis and synthesis. These types of thought processes facilitate learning. Consequently, if you are thinking about it, you are learning it. You will be less likely to go to sleep, daydream, or wonder what you have read if you are concentrating on an outline. As an additional consideration, some repetition (reinforcement) in ESS is necessary in order to (a) facilitate the mastery of study skills as soon as possible and (b) develop them to a more sophisticated level.

The most important benefit of outlining, however, is this. *The mind looks for structure, for category, for concise organization.* It will more quickly grasp material that is clearly and simply organized. Consequently, *you should get the material you will be held responsible for into such a form not only for maximum learning, but for maximum performance on exams as well.*

When many beginning students attempt to read and master college texts in the same way they deal with other forms of reading, they usually meet with little success. This is because they are bombarded with large numbers of abstract concepts, principles, theories, and so forth from their texts and they lack a structured way of organizing this information in an efficient and effective way. Consequently, much if not most of such material has a tendency to go over their heads. If they engage in cramming a day or two before the exam and somehow manage to retain enough material to pass, what they do recall through memorization tends to imprint itself on only short-term memory, which is quickly lost. Their performance on exams tends to be mediocre as well.

In contrast, the textbook usage skills contained in ESS help to provide students with a means of not only passing exams, but obtaining straight A's if they are willing to work hard for them. These skills also help students to retain more material in long-term memory. Since the human mind, as stated earlier, tends to grasp more readily and retain material that is structured, patterned, or ordered, *chapter outlining acts as the capstone to effective textbook usage in that it provides students with a coherent and logical synthesis of all that is contained in a given textbook chapter.* Students who are armed with such comprehensive chapter outlines for all the text material to be included on an exam have a distinct advantage over students who are not.

e. Time Management

As you make use of your textbook usage skills, it will be important to pace yourself carefully to accomplish everything you want to do. In this regard, effective management of your study time is also a crucial skill. Without it, you will not be able to prepare most effectively for the exams you must take in each of your courses. Time is a resource and, like money, property, or other valuable things, can be easily lost if not managed properly. To manage study time more effectively, you will need to implement the following tasks:

> e. Time Management
> Tasks to Perform:
>
> (1) Complete Text Assignments Weekly
>
> (2) Use a Weekly Calendar to Budget Time
>
> (3) Set Priorities to Make Time for Study

(1) Complete Text Assignments Weekly. It is perhaps best to plan the completion of text assignments on a weekly basis. This seems to work particularly well for first-year college students because, although there are exceptions, many if not most survey courses cover about a chapter a week. You now have knowledge of four overlapping textbook usage skills, which, if you develop as explained, will enable you to integrate and master your text assignments. These skills will keep you task-oriented and focused on your goal of academic excellence if you use your time wisely.

(2) Use a Weekly Calendar to Budget Time. To manage time effectively, first develop a weekly calendar with two hours set aside to study for every hour spent in class. This means that if you are taking courses totaling fifteen credit hours, you need to spent thirty hours each week in study. Mastery of the ESS system will take this much time with such a course load, and perhaps even more in the beginning. As you plan your calendar, try to assess the time that you will need to spend with your family, at an outside job if you must work, in recreation and social life, and so on. The mature student realizes that college is a serious commitment and that there are only so many hours in the day and so many days in the week.

(3) Set Priorities to Make Time for Study. If you work at an outside job, have family responsibilities, and are carrying a heavy course load at school, you will experience what sociologists call *role conflict,* and adjustments will have to be made. Perhaps if you have heavy responsibilities in all these areas, you might consider taking a smaller class load next term or cutting back on the hours at your job if you can. However, you must weigh these issues yourself and resolve them in a manner that best meets your priorities and needs. However, *if you truly expect to achieve academic excellence and go as far as your abilities will allow you, then school must be near or at the top of your priority list. In the final analysis, it is only the student who will do this for whom ESS will provide significant benefit.*

STEP 2: CONTENT ORGANIZATION SKILLS

In the next step of ESS, you will learn how to build upon your textbook usage skills to organize effectively the course content that comes from different sources. These include textbooks, class lectures, and collateral reading. **Content organization skills** *involve the development of a comprehensive written outline from all sources of course content.* This comprehensive outline becomes the source document you study from as you prepare for an upcoming exam in a particular course. As you master the skills of pulling everything together and constructing a final outline, such things as textbooks, lecture notes, and collateral readings can be put aside. You will not need them once your comprehensive outline is complete. Your final written outline thus becomes the "blueprint for success" that allows you to excel on each and every exam.

In contrast, some beginning students find themselves in a somewhat frustrating predicament as each exam approaches. Even if they have tried to study as they went along and have not procrastinated by putting things off until the last day or two before the exam, they find themselves sifting and sorting among several different sources of course content in an attempt to pull everything together. For the student who "crams," this can be a frantic experience— "using too little too late"— resulting in an F grade on the exam. However, even under the best of circumstances, the lack of a comprehensive written outline can represent a very inefficient way to prepare for an exam. Consequently, many students who do not use ESS or something like it find themselves on the day before the exam thumbing through a hundred or perhaps even two hundred pages of text or more, sifting through dozens of pages of lecture notes, and, in some cases, needing to know all the pertinent information contained in assigned articles or other forms of collateral reading.

Through the use of ESS, however, you will be spared this sifting and sorting routine. You will also be spared the anxiety that many students feel as the time ticks away and the appointed hour of the exam draws near. *You will have a plan of action and will be equipped with a comprehensive outline, which, once you learn how to develop and use it, will consist of only eight or ten sheets of paper for each major exam.*

When you prepare for final exams, you will again have it much easier than many students because you will have prepared in a focused, task-oriented manner as you went along. *All you will have to do for a comprehensive final exam is pull out the written outlines you saved from each of the previous exams and use them along with the one you developed for the last part of the semester.* Therefore, while some other students, for each final exam, will no doubt be sifting and sorting through four or five hundred pages of required semester readings and perhaps a hundred or more pages of lecture notes, *you will have distilled and condensed everything down to approximately forty sheets of paper or less.* In addition, because of the effort you expend in condensing the course material and developing these outlines as you go along, you already will know the material fairly well and will find it much easier to study for the exam.

Just as the gold miner uses a long trough—a sluice—to separate an ounce or two of gold from tons of rich but muddy soil or silt, you can use the comprehensive written outline to capture all the valuable pieces of information that will appear on an exam. To accomplish this, it is important to acquire and make use of the following skills:

Step 2: Content Organization Skills

a. Use of Preliminary Outlines

b. Constructing the Comprehensive Outline

c. Time Management

d. Summary: Steps 1 and 2

a. Use of Preliminary Outlines

In Step 1: Textbook Usage Skills, you learned how to identify and organize different types of course content for effective learning. After engaging in the skills and tasks of (1) active reading, (2) identification of core material, (3) topical mapping, (4) chapter outlining, and (5) time management, you not only have captured the essence of a given textbook chapter and learned it fairly well, but have also paced yourself in an appropriate way through effective time management.

Assume for the purposes of illustration that most of the courses you are taking (in the first and second year) require about a chapter of reading a week. If you begin on Monday, then by the middle or near the end of the week, you should have completed the text assignment for that week in each of your courses. Each chapter you have completed and outlined, for the purposes of Step 2 of ESS, then becomes a preliminary outline that you will use along with other material to construct your comprehensive outline on a week-by-week basis. To use such preliminary outlines properly, you will need to carry out the following tasks:

a. Use of Preliminary Outlines
    Tasks to Perform:

    (1) Textbook Assignments

    (2) Class Notes

    (3) Collateral Readings

(1) Text Assignments. Suppose, for example, that you begin the semester with a course in which there will be a major exam over the first four textbook chapters in one month's time. To be most successful in preparing for such an exam and others like it, you will need to carry out the following task with your **textbook assignments.** *Each week, the student should (1) complete the reading assignment for that period using textbook usage skills and (2) incorporate this material into the comprehensive outline at that time.*

Research on learning has shown clearly that *writing tends to be an active learning process.* When you write things down, this facilitates learning. Therefore, you will need to take the extra effort to transfer the important material from the text to your comprehensive written outline (in your own words). This will (1) reinforce learning and (2) free you from the more bulky text. You will benefit because everything you will need to know for the exam will be written down in a concise and much more useful form.

(2) Class Notes. In addition to the preliminary outline you develop weekly from text assignments, you will also have weekly preliminary outlines from one and possibly two other basic sources of course content, namely class lectures and collateral readings. Although some college instructors lecture almost exclusively from the text, many will include in their lectures or class discussions a significant amount of additional material that is not found in the textbook. Therefore, for maximum success, you will need to read all appropriate reading assignments before coming to class, and to take comprehensive class notes (see Action Principles for Student Effectiveness 5 and 6). At the end of each week, you should have several pages of class notes from each of the courses you take. **Class notes** *for each course should be consolidated at the end of each week and then integrated into the comprehensive outline at that time.*

(3) Collateral Readings. In some of the courses you take, you will also have **collateral readings,** *assignments in addition to those in the textbook.* Such assignments, also referred to as outside readings, may be of various forms, such as material placed on library reserve, a book of readings you buy as an additional text, material the instructor hands out in class, and so on. Collateral reading, if required for any course, should be handled in exactly the same manner as textbook assignments. It should first be read and outlined, using all the textbook usage skills, and then consolidated on a weekly basis into the comprehensive outline for a particular exam.

b. Constructing the Comprehensive Outline

As you implement the ESS system, you will need to develop a comprehensive written outline for each exam you take in each course. Consequently, in a given semester with a 15-hour course load, you might go through this process fifteen to twenty times or more, depending on the number of exams you have in each course. This portion of Step 2 focuses on the procedures you should use to construct this outline physically in the fastest and easiest way possible. For greatest success, you will need to carry out the following tasks:

> b. **Constructing the Comprehensive Outline**
> **Tasks to Perform:**
>> (1) **Decide on an Outline Model**
>>> (a) **Textbook**
>>> (b) **Class Notes**
>>> (c) **Collateral Readings**
>> (2) **Decide on a Physical Format**
>>> (a) **Letter-Size Paper**
>>> (b) **5″ × 8″ Index Cards**

As you progress through the several weeks of course content material leading up to each exam, you will be integrating the preliminary material you have gleaned from the text, the class notes, and the collateral readings (if applicable) into your comprehensive written outline for each course. **This outline will become the source document from which you will study for the exam.** How to use this outline most effectively to study for the exam will be explained fully in Step 3 of ESS to follow. However, the focus will now be on how to construct the outline for maximum benefit.

(1) Decide on an Outline Model.   To construct your comprehensive outline most effectively, you must first choose the particular source of course content—textbook, class notes, or collateral reading—on which it should be modeled. To best make this decision, *ask yourself the following question with each exam you take in every course: Which source of course content do I think the largest number of exam questions will come from?*

The answer to this question will decide the issue: If you feel most questions will come from the textbook, use the material you have identified and outlined in the text as the **model** for your comprehensive outline. Then, examine your class notes and collateral readings (if applicable) for core material that does not appear in the text and incorporate it into the outline as well. In this manner, you will "have all your bases covered" and, if you have prepared well, very little if anything that is important will be left out. However, if you feel the largest number of test questions will come from class notes, you should use this source of content for your outline model and make adjustments accordingly.

(2) Decide on a Physical Format.   Your next task in regard to the comprehensive outline is to decide on which type of **physical format** to use. This basically is a matter of personal preference. Some students prefer to use standard letter-size paper (with or without lines), and others prefer $5'' \times 8''$ index cards. It is recommended, however, that you use letter-size paper until your skill for outlining is fully developed. When you can successfully transfer all the core material for a major exam from all sources of course content to one side of eight or ten sheets of paper in a legible form, then you will be ready to use index cards if that is your preference.

The first time or two that students develop a comprehensive outline, it is not uncommon for them to have twenty pages or more. If this happens to you, be patient. You will reach full mastery with dutiful application and a little time. In the beginning you may write larger than necessary and will more than likely include things that are not essential. This is to be expected as you sharpen your skills. Keep in mind that it is always better to have too much than not enough in the beginning. The key is to not leave out any core material if you can help it. *With time and practice, you will be able to construct outlines of eight or ten pages, or even less.*

To begin the process of physically writing your comprehensive outline, you need to *have several sheets of letter-size paper. On one, which will become page 1 of the outline, draw a vertical line down the center.* The purpose of this line is to help you learn to be as concise as possible and to write small. *As you write on this piece of paper, you will start at the top on the left side of the line and progress downward until you reach the bottom. Then you will start again at the top of the page on the right side of the line and move toward the bottom again.* In this manner, you will soon discover that each sheet of paper becomes like two, and you can get two to three times as much material on one side of a letter-size sheet than you could have otherwise.

Follow the same procedure with each sheet of paper until your outline of the material for an upcoming exam is complete. If you do decide to switch to index cards at a later time, the line down the middle will not be necessary, given both your mastery of outlining skills and the relatively small size of such cards.

c. Time Management

Effective time management with Step 2 of ESS can be accomplished through the use of the following procedures:

> c. Time Management
> Tasks to Perform:
>> (1) Follow the Two-Day Rule
>>
>> (2) Use a Weekly Study Cycle
>>
>> (3) Construct the Final Outline in Increments

(1) Follow the Two-day Rule. To complete successfully your final outline each time, it is important that you pace yourself carefully and follow **the two-day rule.** For purposes of effective time management, *the comprehensive written outline must be completed no later than two days before the scheduled exam. For final exams given at the end of each semester, all final outlines must be completed by two days before the final exam week or period begins.* Following this rule is necessary to ensure that enough time (the day before each exam) will be available to implement Step 3 of ESS which is yet to be explained.

(2) Use a Weekly Study Cycle. To finish your outline on time, you will need to divide the time you have before a major exam into segments, such as weeks. In fact, it is recommended that you use a weekly study cycle if possible. *At the end of each week, consolidate your reading assignments and class notes and integrate them into the final outline.*

(3) Construct the Final Outline in Increments or Stages. By continuing the use of the weekly study cycle, you will steadily organize content material and construct the final outline in increments or stages as you move toward the day of the exam. This is the most prudent way to study for maximum results. The benefits to you will be increased learning and higher grades.

d. Summary: Steps 1 and 2

Success in any field of endeavor comes to the person who works hard and "works smart." This statement will already apply to you as a college student, once each and every principle, step, and task explained so far in ESS has been fully implemented. In other words, *once you have implemented Steps 1 and 2, you will have demonstrated that you have the maturity, commitment, and discipline to become an exceptional student if you continue in your efforts.* In this regard, you are the most important ingredient in the formula for academic excellence. ESS furnishes only the basic tools you will need.

If the preceding paragraph describes you and these steps have already been completed, let us examine what you have accomplished so far. First, you have put into practice the ten action principles for student effectiveness. Their implementation alone will greatly enhance the grades you receive in your college courses. Next, you have implemented Step 1: Textbook Usage Skills. Consequently, your comprehension and retention of required reading material have been significantly improved. Finally, you have started to use the content organization skills contained in Step 2, which will provide you with a single source document to use for effective and efficient exam preparation.

These are all valuable components of a study strategy that will make you a winner. What you will need is patience and perseverance for the next few weeks and months for all skills to be fully mastered. After you spend a college term or two in conscientious application, these skills will become internalized as competencies and habits, and you will find it much easier to perform successfully in school. NOTE: The going will be slow at first and perhaps even tedious at times. However, once mastery of all ESS skills is attained, you will be amazed at how quickly you can successfully deal with academic material.

STEP 3: EXAM PREPARATION SKILLS

Now it is time to discuss the skills you will need to use on the day before an exam, and during the exam itself, to ensure maximum performance and an A grade. But first, a few words about attitude might be helpful. Sociologists who study attitude formation and how it affects performance have found that the reference groups people choose for themselves play a crucial role in how they approach tasks. A **reference group** is *a group of people that a person refers to consciously or unconsciously as a basis for evaluating life goals and performance.* Consequently, our reference groups are the yardsticks by which we judge our own successes and failures.

Suppose, for example, a group of students at your college or university takes a major exam. At the next class meeting, the instructor gives back the papers with the grades. The first student who receives a paper looks at it, sees the B − recorded there, and with a slight smile thinks, "This means I can make a D the next time and still get by." The second student looks at the grade received, observe a B, and feels very disappointed because it is so low. Although both students received essentially the same grade, they had different attitudes about it because of the reference groups with which they identified. Therefore, if you identify with "A" students, see yourself in your mind's eye as an "A" student, and make every attempt to seek out and associate with "A" students, you will increase your chances of becoming one.

Exam preparation skills form the basis for Step 3 of ESS. Taken as a whole, they will furnish you with an efficient means of integrating everything you have learned previously for maximum performance, assist you in developing an effective strategy for use in an actual test situation, and furnish techniques for overcoming common test-related problems. To acquire these benefits, you will need to learn and implement the following skills:

Step 3: Exam Preparation Skills

a. Final Study Session

b. How to Take a Test

a. Final Study Session

By the time you get to Step 3, your comprehensive written outline has been completed two days before the scheduled exam. All the core content you will be expected to know should be contained in this single, concise document. At this stage, you have no more need of the textbooks, class notes, or collateral readings that are so often spread across dining room tables and bedroom floors throughout America on that notorious night before "it" is to occur—the major exam the next day. For you, all of these images will soon be just faint memories of the way things used to be before ESS. Now, after all the hard work and preparation, you will perhaps say to others, "This is really great. Eight to ten sheets of paper for a major exam. Thirty to thirty-five or forty sheets for a comprehensive final. How could things be much better?"

Well, in truth, things could not be much better for you at this point. You have done your homework, prepared diligently, and learned the material responsibly in increments as you went along. Now you are ready for the final push to victory, the final study session that should result in content mastery and an A on the exam (once ESS is fully mastered). The **final study session** *refers to a concentrated study period with the comprehensive outline the day before the scheduled exam.* Based on norms established by the reports of 2000 first-semester students used in the testing of ESS, *the final study session should require about one to two hours for a major exam (when there are three or more exams per semester), two to three hours for a midterm exam, and three to four hours for a comprehensive final exam. These, of course, are average times that occasionally may need to be expanded for certain courses.* During this period of study, you will need to follow the procedures outlined here for maximum success:

a. Final Study Session
   Tasks to Perform: (Drill and Practice)

   (1) One-Page Review Tests

   (2) Final Review Test

These are the step-by-step instructions you will need to follow for this final session. First, get your comprehensive outline, one or more blank sheets of paper, and something to write with; then go to a quiet place where you will not be disturbed. It is here that you will carry out **drill and practice,** *an intense process in which questions are asked repeatedly and answers given until complete mastery of all material on which you will be tested is demonstrated.* This technique, if used properly, is invaluable because it provides you with an effective way to anticipate practically any question that could be asked on an exam.

To use drill and practice properly, you will need to restate the material contained in the comprehensive outline in the form of questions. This is what educators do when they design test questions for their students. They take essential content and formulate it into various types of questions for exams. When you take the same essential material and ask yourself questions about it, you are engaged in an approximate simulation of what actually will be experienced in the exam. Therefore, to use an expression from the theater world, it is like dress rehearsal before opening night.

This is what you need to do. Take a blank sheet of paper and, using it as a covering, proceed to the first heading on the first page of your outline. Take care to keep everything else covered. Now look at the statement, phrase, or word you see there and make a question out of it. If, for example, you are studying for an American History exam and the first heading is "The Major Causes of the Civil War," then make a mental question, such as "What were the main causes of the Civil War?" You may find it useful to write the questions on a separate sheet of paper for quick reference later.

Try to answer the question without looking at the material hidden by the cover sheet. If necessary, peek at the answer, study it carefully, and then ask the same question again. When you feel you have complete control over this first part of the outline and can answer the question each time, then move on down your outline to the next key heading and handle it in the same manner. Continue this process until you feel you have adequately mastered all the core material contained on the first page. Place checkmarks in the margin of the page as the material is mastered.

(1) One-Page Review Tests. After you have completed the drill and practice procedure with this first part of the outline, go back and perform a review test on the material on the first page. You do this by asking and answering all the pertinent questions you developed, with the cover sheet placed over the answers. Once you can answer *all* such questions, go to the next page of the outline and repeat the procedure. Each succeeding page in the outline should be handled in exactly the same manner and followed by a successful one-page review test *before* drill and practice with an additional page is attempted.

(2) Final Review Test. When you have completed the drill and practice procedure for each page, then perform a final review test on all material in the outline. When you can answer all questions pertaining to the material in the comprehensive outline, you will be ready for the exam scheduled for the next day. In fact, you should earn an A grade at the least, perhaps even score 99 or 100 percent after you have implemented and mastered the entire ESS system.

b. How to Take a Test

Taking a test is an acquired skill just like most other forms of behavior. That is, it can be learned and improved upon with the right information and a little effort. Likewise, deficiencies in test-taking techniques are sometimes partially if not largely responsible for turning what could have been a good performance on an exam into a mediocre one at best. In a few cases, beginning students may even fail an exam because, in part, they do not know some of the essential principles and necesary tasks involved in effective test taking.

Your ESS skills prepare you to deal successfully with either rote recall or critical thought questions. The process you go through in getting to Step 3 forces you to concentrate on the material, analyze it carefully, and then synthesize it into a clear and concise final outline. Therefore, not only do you clearly understand discrete bits of core material such as facts, but you understand the relationships between them as well. You are therefore able to see the big picture. Material that is thoroughly studied in this manner is more likely to imprint itself into long-term memory and contribute to your development as an educated person. Then, as an additional reinforcement, the drill and practice component (memorization) in Step 3 thoroughly encodes everything you will need to know for the next day's test into short-term memory for maximum performance.

Although you will forget much if not most of the particulars asked for on exams, you will nonetheless tend to remember and understand more of the key ideas and concepts for years to come because of the way you prepared. Cramming, in contrast, involves little more than memorization for recognition and identification. The student who uses it as a primary study approach is not only cheated in terms of earning poorer grades, but, more important, is also denied a good education, even though much time and money has gone into an attempt to acquire it.

What you know and your ability to communicate or demonstrate what you know are two separate things. Simply stated, the possession of one should not assume the other. *Exam preparation skills must include not only how to identify and master material that will appear on tests, but how to communicate effectively and demonstrate that knowledge as well. The tangible results of this two-fold process are called "grades."* They tend to follow you as permanent records of your academic achievement for your entire life. Therefore, to improve your success in transferring what you know to a document called a "test" which, together with other tests, will be recorded as a grade, it is important that you understand some of the basic techniques of testing. These, in the order to be discussed, are outlined as follows:

b. **How to Take a Test**
    Tasks to Perform:

    (1) **Objective Exams**

        (a) **Know Types of Questions**

        (b) **Avoid the Formula Fallacy**

        (c) **Read Questions Properly**

        (d) **Use the Deduction Strategy**

    (2) **Essay Exams**

        (a) **Know Types of Questions**

        (b) **Use the Cardinal Rule of Essay Writing**

        (c) **Practice Essay Writing Etiquette**

        (d) **Use the Steps in Writing an Essay**

(1) Objective Exams. *Forms of evaluation that furnish the student with a predetermined number of possible answers or choices with which to demonstrate knowledge of the course material* are **objective exams.** Many instructors prefer this type of test because, although it

can be very time consuming to develop, it can be quickly graded. Some of the more common forms of such tests make use of *multiple-choice, true-false, matching,* or *fill-in-the-blank (completion) items or questions.* Of these, multiple-choice and true-false questions tend to be most popular among college instructors.

Multiple-choice tests, for example, typically employ four or five possible responses that usually are arranged into choices of a., b., c., d., and e. They ask the student to provide the correct or best answer from among a preset number of alternatives. The student, first of all, should **know the different types of questions** that might be asked. Some multiple-choice items measure only memorization and rote recall. With these, the student needs only to recognize or identify the material correctly. Others, however, may measure the student's understanding of the material and his or her ability to think critically with it.

For instance, a multiple-choice question may first state a situation or problem in a sentence or two or even a brief paragraph. Then the student is asked to analyze it and choose the best solution from among several alternatives. Choices such as "all of the above," "none of the above," and "both a. and c. above" are also clues that the instructor is testing for understanding and critical thinking ability. Some students unfamiliar with these more sophisticated forms of multiple-choice questions may regard them as "tricky"; this is what you must prepare yourself for in order to do well in a college or university setting.

A common mistake many students make is to believe **the formula fallacy.** This is *the erroneous belief by some students that intructors use a set number of choices for multiple-choice or true-false items in a particular order.* The instructor supposedly uses a formula of some sort in choosing the correct responses to items on a test. Such mythical formulas take a variety of different forms, but only in the minds of some students. For example, a student may choose a "d." response on a multiple-choice test for little other reason than "it is time for a 'd.'" Because there has not been a "d." answer for nine questions—the student has taken precious test time to go back and count them—the answer must be "d." Likewise, if the student has made four "True" responses in a row, he or she might feel that it is time for a "False," or perhaps even go back and change one of the other "True" answers for balance.

While instructors do see the need to have a variety of different choices as test answers, they rarely if ever use a formula as such. Their primary concern is in choosing test items that are representative of the material on which students will be tested, not in how many of each type of correct response there are or in what order they appear. Consequently, it is not uncommon to see several "a." or "b." or "True" or "False" responses in a row on objective tests. *The best strategy you can use for taking objective tests is to know the material well.* Then you will have the self-confidence to ignore the formula fallacy.

One important skill to use in taking objective tests is **reading questions properly.** To do this, *read each question carefully and completely and then record the first firm impression as the final response.* It is important not to go back and second-guess yourself by changing an answer once a selection has been made. Many beginning students make the mistake of doing this, which often results in lower text scores.

With true-false questions, students should watch for two things in particular. *First, look for absolute statements using words such as "all" "always," "invariably," "none" or "never."* Few things are absolutely one way or another. Therefore, statements stated as absolutes are usually false. *Second, be wary of true-false statements with two or more indepen-*

dent clauses. One may be true while the other is false. This makes the entire statement false. Consider the following true-false item from an economics exam:

> Karl Marx had a class conflict view of history in which the bourgeoisie consisted of the "have-nots", or industrial workers, while the proletariat was represented by the capitalist owners of industry, or "haves."

The first part of the statement, "Karl Marx had a class conflict view of history" is true. However, the terms *bourgeoisie* (in reality "the haves") and *proletariat* (the true "have-nots") have been switched around. Be careful. Such test questions can be deceptive if you do not read them carefully.

In taking objective tests, there are two other common mistakes relating to proper reading that are often made by students. One of these is *underreading*. Take multiple-choice tests for example. Many students read a question until the choice containing the correct answer appears, and then mark it as the final response. The choices that appear after the "right answer" are not read. So, if a student marks "c." as the correct response without having read "d." and "e.," he or she might be in for a surprise when the tests are returned and the correct answer to that question was "e.," which was "both c. and d above."

Likewise, some students overread test questions by reading and rereading them and all the possible choices over and over again. When *overreading* occurs, it is easy to pay undue attention to individual words in each choice and, therefore, take them out of context. This leads to a tendency to misperceive individual words or choices and read things into them that simply are not there. Questions dealt with in this manner are often missed because their original intent has been misconstrued. Therefore, *the best strategy in dealing with questions on objective tests, particularly multiple-choice items, is to read each question once very carefully and then record your final response.*

If you read a question on a test and you do not know the answer, do not dwell on it or worry over it. Instead, skip it and move on. You can come back to it later. It might be that other questions which follow will give you clues as to how to answer one that was skipped or, in some cases, trigger a complete response. If suddenly you realize the answer to a skipped question, you can go back and complete it. Otherwise, wait until the entire test has been completed and then go back and deal with any questions that were skipped.

When you do this, it is helpful to use **the deduction strategy.** This is *a process in which incorrect choices on some types of objective exams are carefully eliminated, so that if guesswork becomes necessary, it involves the fewest alternatives.* This becomes a particularly useful technique on matching and multiple-choice questions. Once all your ESS skills are fully mastered, however, this situation will occur rarely if at all, because you will know all the material.

(2) Essay Exams. In addition to objective exams, there are **essay exams.** These tests *involve forms of evaluation that require the student to demonstrate knowledge of the subject through one or more forms of expository writing.* The student thus is required to give more open-ended answers, as compared with the more close-ended responses that characterize objective tests. Many instructors prefer this evaluation approach because, in addition to tak-

ing little time to prepare, essay exams provide an effective way of assessing writing and critical thinking skills.

Essay questions tend to fit into **two general categories,** those that require little more than recall and description and those that necessitate some analysis and critical thinking. Descriptive essay questions tend to begin with "List," "Discuss," and "Review." Analytical essay questions tend to begin with terms like "Argue," "Justify," "Compare and Contrast," and "Explain."

Descriptive questions typically are *the easier to answer, in that they usually require only a description of an aspect of course content.* For questions that begin with "List," "Describe," "State," and "Review," you are required to recall little more than all the parts that make up a whole, rather than an explanation of why each piece came to be or how the various parts fit together. "List" questions tend to differ from "Describe" and "State" questions only in the sense that they are more specific, such as "List the parts of a business letter" in an English class. In contrast, a "Review" question may be either specific ("Review the causes of the Mexican-American War") or general ("Review the nineteenth century"). However, regardless of whether the question asks you to "List," "Describe," "State," or "Review," be careful not to engage in a detailed explanation or analysis of the elements. This is not what the question is asking for.

"Trace" questions are also descriptive in nature. They imply a sequence or chronological order of things or events in a step-by-step fashion. In some courses, such as history and political science, for example, they may also involve a time frame. The student may need to structure the answer from one point in time to another, as in "Trace the Prohibition movement from its beginning to its demise."

"Discuss" questions tend to be somewhat more difficult than others because they are so general. Unlike questions that usually give you some specifics to work with, such as "List the causes of the Great Depression" in American History or "Describe the parts of a cell" in biology, "Discuss" questions tend to be somewhat more challenging. This is because you have to make the decision regarding what is to be described, and even explained, to some degree. If, for example, you get a question in biology that says, "Discuss the cell," then you have to decide to tell a story in the manner you feel is best. Do you discuss "the parts of the cell," "what a cell looks like," "how it functions and divides," or all three or none of these aspects? The choice is yours. Therefore, the instructor is testing not only what you know, but how well you organize and prioritize information.

"Identify" is another type of descriptive essay question. It asks for a specific type of description in terms of one or more elements of "who, what, where, when, why, and how." The nature of the subject matter to be identified tells you which or how many of these elements to use and in which order to use them. If you were asked to identify "Sri Lanka" in geography, the focus would tend to be on "what" and "where" as you identified it as an island in the Indian Ocean, formerly named Ceylon, that lies off the southeastern tip of India. If you were asked to identify "Sigmund Freud" in psychology, you would first tell "who," then "when," and finally "what" he did to make him such a prominent figure in behavioral science. Answers to "Identify" questions tend to be relatively brief, varying from only one or two sentences to about a page or so.

Analytical questions tend to be *more complex and lengthy than descriptive questions and address the ability of the student to think critically about the course material.* The most straightforward and often the simplest form of analytical question begins with such terms as "Explain," "Cite the reasons for . . . ," or "What were the causes of . . . ?" As such, *explanation questions ask for the causes or reasons that account for something.* If, for example, the question asked in an American History course was "Explain the causes of World War I," The student could satisfy the question in most instances by listing each of the major causes and elaborating on each one in some detail. However, if the question began with the phrase "Analyze the causes of . . . ," the message would be clear that a more sophisticated response was being called for. However, if you have any doubt as to what your instructor means by the term "Explain," ask for some clarification.

If you get an essay question that begins with *"Analyze,"* it is clear that you are being asked to do two things in the following sequence: *(1) identify the important parts of something and (2) show how they are interrelated in forming the whole.* For the first task, it is essential that you prioritize the parts and place the most important element at the top of the list. This shows the instructor that you have thought the question through and understand the "big picture." Suppose your sociology instructor asked you to "Analyze the development of twentieth-century sociology." To accomplish this, you might first describe, in rank order of prominence, the different schools of sociological thought that emerged in this century and then explain how they developed and interfaced with one another to develop the state of sociological knowledge as it is today.

Your ESS skills are essential here because, if you have used the system as explained, you have already prioritized elements of several types of anticipated questions before the time of the test. All that is left to do when you take the test is to convert your outline, which is firmly impressed on your mind, to paragraph form. Consequently, rather than having to use a significant amount of exam time thinking such issues through, you will have already done most of this as you prepared for the test.

"Argue" questions are those in which students are asked to choose a side or position on an issue and support it with good evidence and logic. Usually, the position to be taken is left to the student. The instructor is interested not in which side you take, but in how well you marshall your facts and present them in an organized, persuasive, and logical manner as you plead your case to its conclusion. For such questions, simply memorizing facts through cramming will not help you much. The instructor, when grading such a response, will be just as interested in *how* the facts are organized and argued as in what pieces of information are used.

You can anticipate such questions in the way you use your ESS skills to construct your comprehensive outline. If, for instance, you are taking an economics, history, or political science course, which are noted for both essay exams and "argue" questions, you can focus on key issues and be prepared to argue them for any point of view before you take the test.

This is often a prudent thing to do, because some instructors do not provide students with the luxury of choosing which side of an issue or argument to take. Instead, they may use one or more questions on an essay exam that begin with "Justify," "Defend," "Prove," or "Show that." These are *questions in which the instructor has predetermined the side of an argument the student is to take and then support with good evidence and logic.* To illustrate: you might take a course in history in which the instructor asks you on an exam to "Justify the bombing of Pearl Harbor from the Japanese point of view." Again, this would measure not only your command of the facts and issues surrounding a question, but your ability to develop a particular line of argumentation to plead a case.

Another form of exam question is one that begins with "Compare and contrast." This is *a question that instructs students to establish the extent to which two or more things are similar to and different from one another.* This is a popular type of question among instructors who make use of essay tests because it is an excellent measure of how much students know about two different issues or topics and their ability to compare them in an organized way. Sometimes two things will have a fair balance of similarities and differences. However, in other instances the two may be almost completely alike or dissimilar. Therefore, students who know the material well will be able to structure their answers to reflect the true situation between the two or more things being compared.

There is a **cardinal rule of essay writing.** *Always assume that the reader (the instructor) knows absolutely nothing about the topic on which you are writing and that, therefore, you will teach this person everything he or she will ever know on the subject.* In placing yourself in the role of teacher and, through your essay, developing a lesson for the reader, you will be sensitive to the concerns of the reader. Too many times students assume that the instructor will "know what I mean" by a response. This often leads to imprecise essay writing, as well. If, however, you take the attitude that you will teach someone everything you know about something in a straightforward, organized, and clear manner, you will tend to do much better on these types of exams.

In addition, there are other rules that together comprise the **etiquette of essay writing.** Some of the more important of these are:

(a) *Arrive on time for the exam.* Not only is it disruptive when someone is late, but students generally need every minute afforded them to complete the exam.

(b) *Come prepared with two pens (in case one runs out of ink) and plenty of writing paper.* In some classes, your instructor will require you to write your responses in a "blue book" that usually is available at any college bookstore. Writing an essay exam in pencil is not acceptable to most instructors.

(c) *Write in a neat and legible fashion.* Your instructor will be reading dozens and possibly a couple of hundred of exams. Be sensitve to this situation and show consideration.

(d) *Avoid using inappropriate language and tone.* Slang and colloquial expressions are to be avoided (except for emphasis, enclosed in quotation marks) and profanity or "cute" attempts at humor must never be used. Essay writing is formal writing and should be handled with decorum.

(e) *Write in complete sentences and in paragraph form.* Such things as phrases, outlines, and diagrams usually are inappropriate on essay exams unless specified by the instructor.

In preparing for an essay exam, it is important to know and use *the steps in writing an essay* and how to manage time effectively as you go through them. These steps are:

(a) *Read the entire exam.* If your instructor allows you to make choices among the questions to answer, do so at this time. This entire process, in most cases, should take only about five minutes.

(b) *Construct an outline for answering each major question.* This will help to organize your thoughts and provide you with a structure for writing. In most instances, it should take no more than five to ten minutes to outline the entire exam. As a guide, spend no more than ten percent of the total time allowed for the exam on outlining. Through the use of ESS, this will be simplified tremendously because you will have a complete outline of the material in your head going into the exam.

(c) *Write the answers and complete the exam.* As this is done, keep track of the time and allocate the necessary amount of time to each question. Be sure to prioritize the questions so that the largest amount of time is spent on those which will count most. With longer and more complex essay questions, make sure you include an introduction (how the response is to be organized), a thesis (the body of the essay in which you state your case), and a close (a summary and conclusions).

(d) *Review the exam.* If there is time remaining when you finish, review what you have written. Check for complete sentences, proper spelling, and correct punctuation. Making minor corrections like these will improve the look of your exam and the way it reads.

STEP 4: DIAGNOSTIC FOLLOW-UP

The last step in ESS is designed to provide you with the means to monitor your progress with the study principles, skills, and tasks so that after the test, you can determine why you missed certain questions. **Diagnostic follow-up,** therefore, *is a posttest method of retracing steps taken in exam preparation to discover exactly why any test questions were missed, which ESS steps and skills were involved, and what actions are required to further sharpen skills and improve performance.* By using this diagnostic component, you will be able to learn from the test itself how to study more effectively next time. Consequently, if you use the first three steps of ESS to prepare for an exam and then use this fourth step to test your level of skill usage for future improvement, academic success will be assured.

Step 4 involves the performance of three tasks in the following sequence:

Step 4: Diagnostic Follow-up

a. **Schedule Appointment to Go Over the Exam**

b. **Use Academic Tool Kit to Evaluate Performance**

c. **Implement Action Plan for Improvement**

The first few times you implement ESS, it will be necessary to carry out the step of diagnostic follow-up. *It is recommended that it be used in all courses at least for the first semester in which the ESS system is initiated.* However, once it is clear that your study skills are developing and performance on exams shows significant improvement, the use of the diagnostics component of ESS can be abandoned. So, as mastery of the skills is obtained, it will become an optional step.

a. Schedule Appointment to Go Over the Exam

Shortly after the exam is taken, contact your instructor and **schedule an appointment to go over the test.** If you are attending an auditorium class in a major university, you may need to make this appointment with a teaching assistant. You will find that most instructors will oblige this request and will be pleased to assist you. They will be impressed that you are using a system like ESS and are conscientious about your studies. However, if for some reason you meet with some resistance (maybe because the instructor is unfamiliar with ESS), explain clearly to your teacher what you are trying to accomplish. This should be sufficient to take care of such a problem in most cases. *Make sure that your instructor understands what you are doing and why you are doing it.* Your intent is to record *only* the content you missed, not the test question or an instructor's test. *If for some reason your explanation is unconvincing, show your instructor this passage from ESS.* This, in most cases, should resolve the matter. *Your instructors want you to succeed. However, tests are often difficult and time consuming to develop. So care must be exercised that they not be allowed to get out and circulate among those students who might be tempted to cheat.*

b. Use Academic Tool Kit to Evaluate Performance

After you have examined your performance on the test and recorded the content you missed, be sure to go home or to the library and make use of your **academic tool kit.** For the purposes of diagnostic follow-up, this represents *all sources of course content used to prepare for the exam.* The tool kit contains five useful elements needed to assess exam performance: (1) the textbook, (2) all class notes, (3) all collateral reading assignments, (4) the comprehensive written outline, and (5) a complete written copy of ESS. With these tools, you will be able to ascertain why each question was missed (in terms of inadequate skill usage) and, therefore, what you will need to do next time to increase skills and improve performance.

As you begin to analyze the content that you missed on the exam, it will be necessary to set up the **action plan.** This is *a written document that pinpoints (1) areas of content missed on an exam along with (2) areas of deficient skill usage, so that such skills can be developed more fully for the next exam.* To begin, get a blank sheet of paper and write "Action Plan" across the top. Then, near the top of the sheet on the left side, write the heading "Content Missed." Finally, write another heading, "ESS step involved," near the top of the right side of the sheet. Now your Action Plan document has been formatted and you are ready to begin. As you go over the material that you missed, you will need to perform the following tasks:

   b. Use Academic Tool Kit to Evaluate Performance (why questions were missed and what skills need improvement)

   Tasks to Perform:

(1) Complete the Action Plan Document

(2) Use the Reverse-Order Diagnostic Strategy

(1) Complete the Action Plan Document. We will assume that your Action Plan document has been formatted and is ready. So let us begin the diagnostic follow-up. When you prepared for the exam, the first three steps of ESS were used in ascending order: Step 1, Step 2, and Step 3. The content for the exam was continuously condensed, refined, and reinforced until the day of the test arrived and you took the exam. With the diagnostic follow-up, the process is reversed. Consequently, with each area of content you missed on the exam, you will trace back through what you did in descending or reverse order: Step 3, Step 2, and Step 1. In this respect, you will be operating in a "troubleshooting" or diagnostic capacity.

(2) Use the Reverse-Order Diagnostic Strategy. This troubleshooting approach is called the **reverse-order diagnostic strategy.** It involves *retracing steps used in exam preparation in reverse order (3, 2, 1) so that the whys involved in missing certain questions can be clearly identified.* Once this is done, you will know which study skills are being used correctly and, likewise, which ones need more work. Part A of this process is outlined here:

Reverse-Order Diagnostic Strategy: Part A

Starting with ESS Step 3: Tasks to Perform

1. Question or content missed is identified and noted on Action Plan sheet under heading "Content Missed";

2. Final comprehensive outline is examined;

3. If the content material in the question missed is in the comprehensive outline, there are *two reasons* that the question may have been missed:

    a. Inadequate use of Exam Preparation Skills contained in ESS Step 3, or

    a. Inadequate use of Content Organization Skills contained in ESS Step 2;

4. Notation of reason that question was missed is placed on Action Plan sheet under heading "ESS Step Involved."

Let us now consider an example. Suppose as you examined the test, the first question missed was question No. 8. Write down the core material you missed in a word or phrase under "Content Missed" on your Action Plan sheet. Then consult the tool from your academic tool kit used at Step 3 in ESS. This will be your comprehensive written outline. Is the content you missed on that question contained in the outline? If it is, this will tell you one of two things. First, you may have been overconfident and did not properly use the ESS skill of "drill and practice." If this was what happened, you did not follow through, and something called question No. 8 "slipped through the cracks." So you write "Step 3" under the heading on the right side of your action plan sheet, "ESS Step Involved." Next time, you will know you have to work more diligently on the exam preparation skills contained in Step 3.

The only other explanation, if the content missed in the question is on the outline, is that inadequate information was placed on the final outline. For example, if the question missed dealt with a concept and it was on the outline, but the definition and examples relating to it were not included, then you might not have had enough information to deal with. So, you would write "Step 2" (Content Organization Skills) under the heading "ESS Step Involved." Next time, you will need to work on your outlining skills and include more specific material in the outline. When you construct your outline next time, take care to include perhaps some of your analytical summaries of elaboration material from the text in the final outline. In this manner, you will have more elaboration from which to better understand the core material contained in the final outline.

Let us now proceed to the second phase of the reverse-order diagnostic strategy. It is to be used whenever Part A is not sufficient in identifying the reason that a particular question or area of course content was missed on an exam. In this regard, Part B of this process is summarized as follows:

Reverse-Order Diagnostic Strategy: Part B

Proceeding to ESS Steps 2 and 1: Tasks to Perform

1. **Question or content missed on test is not found in the comprehensive outline used to prepare for the exam in ESS Step 3. Therefore, you must troubleshoot elsewhere.**

2. **Textbook (your first source of course content) is examined.**

3. **If the content material contained in the question missed is in the textbook, there are *two reasons* why the question may have been missed:**

    a. **Inadequate use of Content Organization Skills contained in ESS Step 2, or**

    b. **Inadequate use of Textbook Usage Skills contained in ESS Step 1;**

4. **Notation of reason that question was missed is placed on the Action Plan sheet under the heading "ESS Step Involved";**

5. **If the reason the question was missed cannot be determined through an examination of the text, turn next to the class notes (another source of course content) and repeat Tasks 2 through 4 in sequence;**

6. **If the reason the question was missed cannot be determined through an examination of the class notes, turn finally to any assigned collateral readings (a final source of course content) and repeat Tasks 2 through 4 in sequence.**

Suppose, for example, you implemented Part A of the diagnostic follow-up and the content contained in question No. 8 cannot be found in your final outline. It simply is not there. Then you implement Part B. You begin by examining one or more other elements in the academic tool kit that were used at Step 2 of ESS (Content Organization Skills). Start with your textbook. If the material you answered incorrectly in question No. 8 is in your text and you did identify it as core material through Strategic Highlighting, then you have a "Step 2" problem, Content Organization Skills (outlining). You used your Step 1 skills correctly and identified the core material pertaining to the question missed. However, you did not transfer this material from the preliminary outline in the text to the final written outline during Step 2 of ESS. So you make the appropriate "Step 2" notation in the Action Plan under the heading "ESS Step Involved."

If, when you consult the textbook, the material missed on question No. 8 is there, but you did not identify and record it as core material through Strategic Highlighting, then you missed the question for another reason. You have a "Step 1" problem because inadequate use was made of textbook usage skills. Specifically, you will need to work on the Step 1 skills of Active Reading, Identification of Core Material and the Topical Mapping task of Strategic Highlighting.

What if the content material contained in question No. 8 is not found in the textbook? Then you need to consult your class notes. If you find what you are looking for in these notes, but this material was not transferred to the final outline, then you made inadequate use of the ESS Step 2 skills. Consequently, you will need to make the appropriate notation on your Action Plan sheet and work more diligently next time on your Content Organization Skills related to the development of the comprehensive outline.

If the material in the question missed was not found in either the text or the class notes, then you will have to troubleshoot further. It might be that you were absent the day those notes were given, your attention lapsed for a few minutes that day, or you just need to work on "active listening" in class. Another possibility might be a collateral reading assignment. The question might have been based on this source of course content. If that is the case, you can trace this back by using the same procedure already mentioned in regard to the textbook. The same ESS steps and skills apply in this case as well.

Each area of content you miss on an exam is to be handled in the same manner as question No. 8 mentioned above. By conducting the two-part technique of reverse-order diagnostic strategy on all your exam performances until mastery of all ESS skills is acquired, academic excellence will be yours and "A" grades will take care of themselves. The only other element you will need to implement for total success is explained below.

c. Implement Action Plan for Improvement

Once the diagnostic follow-up is completed, your Action Plan document becomes your guide as you work further on developing all the ESS skills to a mastery level. As you examine this completed document, you will notice that each item of content missed has been identified along with the category of skills representing the reason it was missed on the test. In other words, the reason you missed a given test item will be listed under the heading "ESS Step Involved" on the plan: Step 1 (Textbook Usage Skills), Step 2 (Content Organization Skills), or Step 3 (Exam Preparation Skills).

Once completed, *you can use the Action Plan to pinpoint exactly the specific skill or skills involved in each item of content you missed.* With care and concentration on your part, you can even identify which specific tasks under each skill were not carried out properly. In this manner, you will know precisely which areas of skill usage you are performing well and which areas need some additional work. With a little time and diligent application, you will be able to achieve the mastery level with all of the ESS skills. By being equipped with the ESS system, you should be able to obtain success in any academic endeavor.

MASTERING ESS: HOW SKILL-BASED LEARNING WORKS

In many respects, learning academic skills takes place in much the same way as acquiring other important skills. The key ingredients are commitment, regular practice, and hard work. Few if any professional athletes, corporate executives, great inventors and scholars, or leaders in any field obtain their level of success through native talent. They all work hard to achieve excellence and recognition. It is not handed to them. In fact, it was Thomas Alva Edison who said, "Genius is 1 percent inspiration and 99 percent perspiration."

Success in learning skills to accomplish almost anything also requires a plan, a course of action. Louis Pasteur once said, "Chance favors the prepared mind." In regard to academic skills, your plan will be ESS. It requires only dedicated work to implement.

As you put ESS into practice, it may be helpful to know how skill-based learning works to ensure your success. In essence, we progress through **four stages of learning** to achieve mastery at practically anything. These same four levels tend to apply whether skills to be learned are cognitive (intellectual), psychomotor (physical), or a combination of both.

The learning of a new skill begins at what some learning theorists call the "unconscious lack of skill" level. Then we progress through conscious lack of skill and, with the benefit of some learning experiences, reach the conscious skill level. Finally, after a period of practical application, we reach the level of unconscious skill, or mastery learning. These levels are briefly examined, along with an explanation of how to take advantage of ESS: Advanced Applications once mastery of the entire ESS system is achieved.

Mastering ESS: How Skill-Based Learning Works

a. The Four Stages of Learning

b. ESS: Advanced Applications

a. The Four Stages of Learning

(1) Unconscious Lack of Skill. The first stage of learning is often **unconscious lack of skill.** It occurs *when a person (1) does not know that a certain skill is required to perform a task and (2) does not possess it.* Some entering college students are not aware of the many skills that will be required of them in order to succeed and excel in school. Indeed, such an unconscious lack of ability can have a somewhat shocking impact when such students realize that college is not a continuation of high school. This realization often begins for these students when the grades from their first college exams are made available.

(2) Conscious Lack of Skill. Many entering college students, however, begin at the **conscious lack of skill** level in regard to their study skills. *This involves the realization by the individual that deficiencies exist in certain skill areas or that new skills need to be learned.* Many if not most entering freshmen have the background and maturity to know that college is not simply the thirteenth grade and that much more will be required of them as they pursue higher education. Indeed, it is fairly common for many students to enter college with some uncertainty and anxiety about the challenges that lie ahead. However, unlike college students in the past, you will have ESS to use in mastering necessary study skills.

(3) Conscious Skill.   When a person in a skill-based learning situation first tries to implement new skills, this is conscious skill usage. At this learning stage, **conscious skill** *refers to the process in which, as a new skill is acquired, the learner must consciously think about how the skill is to be used as it is being practiced.* Do you remember learning how to swim or drive a car, and how awkward that was? As you apply ESS to your college courses, you will go through a similar learning experience. You will be progressing through the conscious skill level of learning for the first few months. This will require conscious thought on your part as you implement and become comfortable with all the steps, skills, and tasks you will need to perform. Mistakes will be made. Frustration will occur. At times, progress may seem slow and tedious.

Do not be surprised if the first time you take a test after having used ESS you do little or no better than before. Just as you had to struggle with learning to swim, drive a car, and other relatively simple skills, you will also have to "pay your dues" in learning to be an excellent student. When you learn successfully how to do most anything worthwhile in life, it requires time and effort. It is because you have the desire to achieve the goal that you are willing to meet the requirements necessary for success. If you are serious in your goal to succeed and excel as a college student, it will be worth the time spent in mastering ESS.

(4) Unconscious Skill.   The final level of skill-based learning is **unconscious skill.** This is *mastery level learning in which the skill or skills learned have become internalized and are used habitually without the need for conscious thought.* Study skills, like most endeavors, involve a "learning curve" that includes a certain amount of time and effort necessary for full proficiency. For most college students, the learning curve required to achieve full mastery of the ESS system will take approximately six months to one year. However, *when ESS is first implemented, improvements in study skills will be apparent, in most cases, within a few short weeks.* For most students during the first semester of use it is fairly common to see an increase in grade performance of about a letter grade or more beyond that which they might have otherwise received.

Nonetheless, ESS must be implemented as a total system to be fully effective. Use of only certain parts of it, while perhaps beneficial to a limited degree, will significantly reduce the potential benefits. It should also be noted that *ESS should not be implemented in the middle of an exam cycle.* If you first find out about this system two or three weeks before a major exam, do not attempt to use the entire system for that test and try to play "catch up." Do the best you can using the techniques you have used before, plus the ten ESS action principles. Then implement the entire ESS system for the next exam as soon as the period of preparation for that exam starts.

b. ESS: Advanced Applications

As a total system for academic success, ESS works so well that after one year you may be able to use all skills as a total system in a streamlined form for advanced students. This should not be attempted, however, unless you are sure all skills in the entire system have been completley mastered. A good rule of thumb here might be grade-point average. *When you are consistently performing at the level necessary for inclusion on the dean's list, you may then proceed to* **ESS: Advanced Applications.**

Once your academic performance is at this level, here are the streamlined techniques that will be effective. You may choose to *use a six-inch ruler as a skimming device as you read text assignments.* Some students even learn to use a finger. Because the textbook usage skills in Step 1 should be fully mastered by this time, *the distinction between core material and elaboration will come automatically.* If you are typical of many students, core material will almost leap out at you as you read. *You can then have a notepad handy literally to construct a final outline of the text as you read along.*

Your outlining skills should also be developed by this time to the point that *separate in-text outlining will become unnecessary.* The same can be said of skills such as strategic highlighting and analytical summary. *You will still use all the skills, but in a more advanced and efficient application. Analytical summaries of elaboration material will still be made, but written only once in the final outline as necessary.*

When you begin to use such a streamlined application of ESS, it probably will then be necessary to *use assigned text material as the model for the comprehensive final outline in all courses.* Since more and more reading material will be required as you move into more advanced courses, this will tend to be a natural transition and a very logical one to make. Instructors in the more advanced courses at junior, senior, and graduate levels tend to lecture less and place more emphasis on reading assignments and independent study. Typically, the 300 to 500 pages assigned in each course to first- and second-year students become 500 to 800 or more pages for juniors and seniors. First-year graduate students often are required to read 1000 to 2000 pages or more for each course, and doctoral students, depending on the field, are often expected to read much more. Consequently, *ESS will be invaluable should you decide to complete a baccalaureate or higher degree. Once mastery has occurred, ESS can take you as far as you wish to go in higher education.*

To conclude, the author would like to wish you every success as you pursue your studies in the months and years ahead. By reading this far, you have been exposed to a resource that the author and thousands of others would have liked to have used when we first entered college years ago. Many of us, perhaps like you to this point, never had anyone tell us in a concise, step-by-step manner how to study. We had to "fly by the seat of our pants" and learn by trial and error. You, fortunately, can be different. ESS represents a key to a very large and important door. On the other side lies what could be your future, and a bright one at that. Use it.

As an educator, I am always interested in students and how they are getting along. Therefore, as you implement ESS, feel free to write me and let me know how you are doing. My address is given below. I will make every effort to respond to your letter personally as soon as possible.

Dr. James K. Semones
San Jacinto College
Dept. of Sociology
5800 Uvalde
Houston, TX 77049

REFERENCES

Adler, M., and C. Van Doren. *How to read a book.* New York: Simon and Schuster, 1972.

Anderson, T. H. *Another look at the self-questioning study technique* (Technical Educational Report No. 6). Champaign, Ill.: University of Illinois, Center for the Study of Reading, 1978.

Apps, J. W. *Study skills for adults returning to school.* New York: McGraw-Hill, 1982.

Baddeley, A. *Your memory: A user's guide.* New York: Macmillan, 1982.

Bailey, R., and N. Hankins. *Psychology of effective living.* 2d ed. Prospect Heights, Ill.: Waveland Press, 1984.

Beck, A. Cognitive approaches to stress. In *Principles and practice of stress management,* R. L. Woolfolk and P. M. Lehrer. ed. New York: Guilford Press, 1984.

Bloom, B. S., ed. *Developing talent in young people.* New York: Ballentine, 1985.

Boocock, S. S. *An introduction to the sociology of learning.* Boston: Houghton Mifflin Company, 1972.

Bower, G. H. 1970. Organizational factors in memory. *Cognitive Psychology* 1:18–46.

Bower, G. H. 1981. Mood and memory. *American Psychologist* 36:129–148.

Bower, G. H., and P. R. Cohen. Emotional influences in memory and thinking: Data and theory. In *Affect and cognition,* ed. M. S. Clark and S. T. Fiske. Hillsdale, N.J.: Lawrence Erlbaum Associates, 1982.

Brewer, W. F. and J. R. Pani. The structure of human memory. In *The psychology of learning and motivation,* Vol. 17, ed. G. H. Bower. New York: Academic Press, 1984.

Brown, A., J. C. Campione, and C. R. Barclay. 1979. Training self-checking routines for estimating test readiness: Generalizations from list learning to prose recall. *Child Development* 50:501–512.

Burka, J. B., and L. Yuen. *Procrastination.* Reading, Mass.: Addison-Wesley, 1983.

Carver, R. P. Speed readers don't read; they skim. *Psychology Today* (August 1972) 23–30.

Chase, W. G., and K. A. Ericsson. Skilled memory. In *Cognitive skills and their acquisition,* ed. J. R. Anderson. Hillsdale, N.J.: Lawrence Erlbaum Associates, 1981.

Commitment to excellence. Lombard, Ill.: Great Quotations, 1984.

Davis, R. A., and C. C. Moore. 1935. Methods of measuring retention. *Journal of General Psychology* 12:144–155.

Deffenbacker, J. L. 1978. Worry, emotionality and task generated interference in test anxiety: An empricial test of attentional theory. *Journal of Educational Psychology* 70:253–263.

Eddy, J., B. Martin, and J. Semones. *Adult learning and program development: From psychosocial theory to social policy.* Minneapolis: Burgess/ Alpha Editions, 1983.

Ennis, R. H. 1985. Critical thinking and the curriculum. *National Forum* 65:28–30.

Entwistle, D. R. 1960. Evaluations of study skills courses: A review. *Journal of Educational Research* 53:243–251.

Feder, B. *The complete guide to taking tests.* Englewood Cliffs, N.J.: Prentice-Hall, 1979.

Flavell, J. H. *Cognitive development.* 2d ed. Englewood Cliffs, N.J.: Prentice-Hall, 1985.

Flavell, J. H. and H. M. Wellman. Metamemory. In *Perspectives on the development of memory and cognition,* ed. R. V. Kail and J. W. Hagen. Hillsdale, N.J.: Lawrence Erlbaum Associates, 1977.

Gladstone, G. A. 1960. Study behavior of gifted stereotype and non-stereotype children. *Personnel and Guidance Journal* 38:470–474.

Grassick, P. *Making the grade.* New York: Arco Publishing, 1983.

Great quotations. Lombard, Ill.: Great Quotations, 1984.

Green, G. W. *Getting straight A's.* Secaucus, N.J.: Lyle Stuart, 1985.

Hay, J. E., and C. A. Lindsay. 1969. The working student: How does he achieve? *Journal of College Student Personnel* 10:109–114.

Herbert, W. 1983. Remembrance of things partly. *Science News* 124 (24):378–381.

Houston, J. P. *Fundamentals of learning and memory* 2d ed. New York: Academic Press, 1981.

Johnson, M. P. and E. J. Walsh, 1978. Grade inflation or better comprehension. *Teaching Sociology* 5:363–378.

Kaplan, R. M., S. M. McCordick, and M. Twitchell. 1979 Is it the cognitive or the behavioral component which makes cognitive-modification effective in test anxiety? *Journal of Counseling Psychology* 26:371–377.

Lavin, D. E. *The prediction of academic performance.* New York: Russel Sage Foundation, 1965.

Liebert, R. M., and L. W. Morris. 1967. Cognitive and emotional components of test anxiety: A distinction and some initial data. *Psychological Reports* 20:975–978.

Marks, M. B. 1966. Improve reading through better format. *Journal of Educational Research* 60:147–151.

Martindale, C. *Cognition and consciousness.* Homewood, Ill.: Dorsey Press, 1981.

McClelland, D. C. 1985. How motives, skills, and values determine what people do. *American Psychologist* 40:812–825.

Mishkin, M., and T. Appenzeller. 1987. The anatomy of memory. *Scientific American* 256:80–89.

Millman, J., and W. Pauk. *How to take tests.* New York: McGraw-Hill, 1969.

Morris, L. W., M. A. Davis, and C. H. Hutchings. 1981. Cognitive and emotional components of anxiety: Literature review and a revised worry-emotionality scale. *Journal of Educational Psychology* 73:541–555.

Morris, W., ed. *The American heritage dictionary of the English language.* Boston: Houghton Mifflin, 1976, p. 1001.

Neisser, U. 1981. John Dean's memory: A case study. *Cognition* 9:1–22.

Niple, M. L. 1968. The relationship of different study methods to immediate and delayed comprehension. Ph.D. diss., Ohio State University.

Palmer, S. E. 1975. The effects of contextual scenes on the identification of objects. *Memory and Cognition* 3:519–526.

Pauk, W. 1965. Study skills and scholastic achievement, *Reading Teacher* 19:180–182.

Powell, W. J., and S. M. Jourard. 1963. Some objective evidence of immaturity in underachieving college students. *Journal of Counseling Psychology* 10:276–282.

Pressey, L. C., and S. L. Pressey. *Essential preparation for college.* New York: Holt, Rinehart and Winston, 1932.

Preston, R. C. 1948. The reading habits of superior college students. *Journal of Experimental Education* 16:196–202.

Raaijmakers, J. G. W., and R. M. Shiffrin. 1981. Search of associative memory. *Psychological Review* 88:93–134.

Reed, S. K. *Cognition.* Monterey, Calif.: Brooks/ Cole, 1982.

Rogers, C. R. *On becoming a person.* Boston: Houghton Mifflin, 1961.

Robinson, F. P. *Effective study.* 4th ed. New York: Harper & Row, 1970.

Rivin, H. N., D. M. Fraser, and M. R. Stern. *The first years in college: Preparing students for a successful college career.* Boston: Little, Brown and Company, 1965.

Rogers, G. W. 1959. Lecture listening skills: Their nature and relation to achievement. Unpublished Doctoral Dissertation, Ohio State University.

Sarason, I. G. 1984. Stress, anxiety and cognitive interference: Reactions to tests. *Journal of Personality and Social Psychology* 46:929–938.

Sarason, I. G., B. R. Sarason, D. E. Keefe, B. E. Hayes, and E. N. Shearin. 1986. Cognitive interference: Situational determinants and traitlike characteristics. *Journal of Personality and Social Psychology* 51:215–226.

Selig, M. E. P. 1970. On the generality of the laws of learning. *Psychological Review* 77:406–418.

Smith, S. M., A. M. Glenberg, and R. A. Bjork. 1978. Environmental context and human memory. *Memory and Cognition* 6:342–355.

Shaw, P. 1961. Teaching reading skills at college. *School and Society* 89:121–123.

Summer, R. 1968. The social psychology of cramming. *Personnel and Guidance Journal* 47:104–109.

Thomas, E. L., and H. A. Robinson. *Improving reading in every class: A sourcebook for teachers.* Boston: Allyn & Bacon, 1972.

Thompson, R. F. 1986. The neurobiology of learning and memory. *Science* 233:941–947.

Tresselt, M. E. 1966. A preliminary study of factors in learning in a how-to-study course. *Journal of Psychology* 64:91–93.

Trabasso, T., and G. H. Bower, 1968. *Attention in learning.* New York: Wiley, 1968.

Tryon, G. S. 1980. The measurement and treatment of test anxiety. *Review of Educational Research* 50:343–372.

Van Zoost, B. L., and B. T. Jackson. 1974. Effects of self-monitoring and self-administered reinforcement on study behaviors. *Journal of Educational Research* 67:216–218.

Vernon, P. E. 1962. The determinants of reading comprehension. *Educational and Psychological Measurements* 22:269–286.

Wallach, M. A., and C. W. Wing, Jr. *The talented student.* New York: Holt, Rinehart and Winston, 1969.

Zivian, M., and R. Darjes. 1983. Free recall by in-school and out-of-school adults: Performance and metamemory. *Developmental Psychology* 19:513–520.